Beyond Survival

Beyond Survival
(To Eternity)

*Growing Spiritually Via
The Thirteen Principles*

by
Rabbi Ezriel Tauber

written by
Yaakov Astor

ISBN 1-878999-15-X Hardcover
ISBN 1-878999-16-8 Softcover

Copyright © 1994 by Shalheves.

All rights reserved. No part of this publication may be reproduced in any form or by any means, including photocopying, without the written permission of the copyright holder.

Printed in Israel

For a free catalogue or direct sales (individual or wholesale), contact:

Shalheves
PO Box 361
Monsey, NY 10952
Phone: 914-356-3515
Fax: 914-425-2094

"... her flashes are like the flashes of fire, the flame of the Eternal One (*Shalheves Kah*)."
Shir HaShirim 8:6

CONTENTS

Introduction	9
Note To The Reader	13
1. The Thirteen Principles	17
I Believe	20
Perfect Faith	27
Knowledge Today	32
Summary	39
2. The Creator	43
This Moment	44
Bitachon	48
3. Oneness And The Soul	55
Body And Soul	57
Who Am I?	62
Summary	68
4. Prayer	71
The Global Effect	78
5. The Message	89
Moshe Rabbenu	95
Belief and Biblical Criticism	98
Nothing New Under The Sun	101

6. Justice	**107**
He Who Fashions The Heart Is Just	109
Reward And Punishment	116
7. The Coming of the Messiah	**123**
The Teshuva Prophecy	130
8. Life Recycling Life	**139**
Citizenship	147
9. The Formula For Survival	**155**
Bitachon And Chisayon	156
Bitachon in the End of Days	164
Shalheves: Enhancing Lives Through Meaning and Torah	**173**

Beyond Survival

Introduction

According to a statistical study, only one percent of people actually think. Four percent of people think they think. And ninety-five percent of people would rather die than think.

If we reflect on our lifestyle we may find that much of it causes us to be classified in the latter category. How often are we happy to just follow the crowd? How many times are we more than content to tranquilize our day-to-day pain rather than to address it at its source? How often do we resist change because we do not allow ourselves to really stop and reflect deeply and penetratingly into the direction our lives have taken?

We live in a confused, chaotic world, one which continually draws us deeper into the vortex of its manifest chaos. A person who does not think has no ability to resist the powerful undertow of society's magnetic urgings which beckon him ever deeper into the darkening abyss. Even those few who do endeavor to become thinkers are restricted because their thought processes have already been shaped by a confused world. They may spend their time thinking, but in reality they only think they think.

To gain clarity one must actively turn oneself into a genuine thinker; a meditator upon objective reality. The Thirteen Principles are anchored in objective reality. Succinct and to the point they form a single, cohesive structure which encompasses reality in its entirety. One who wants to be a true thinker must be grounded in these Principles.

This book is written for thinkers and the rest of us who want to become thinkers. The Thirteen Principles, meditated upon properly, will naturally produce a penetrating, soulful

Beyond Survival

reflection which can help us deal with the most difficult and confusing situations we find ourselves in—be they family relationships, raising children, making a living, surviving a crisis, etc. Truly, then, what you hold in your hands is a survival guide. Used wisely, again and again, it will not let you down. In fact, it will eventually take you beyond survival and help you turn every life difficulty into a self-replenishing wellspring of renewal and growth.

I want to again acknowledge my debt of gratitude to Yaakov Astor, the writer of this book and our previous six. He possesses the unique ability to extract the depth of my ideas and present them in the clearest, most readily digestible manner. In this book, Yaakov received welcomed editorial feedback from Moshe Efros of Cleveland Heights, and Shmuel Goldstein of Monsey. Their efforts helped fine tune the manuscript.

Finally, I would like to express my gratitude—which, in actuality, is incapable of expression—to my family. May this book and my other life's work truly serve, to whatever small degree possible, as a tribute to the sacrifice and love of those who support me.

E.T.

שלשה עשר עקרים

א. אֲנִי מַאֲמִין בֶּאֱמוּנָה שְׁלֵמָה, שֶׁהַבּוֹרֵא יִתְבָּרַךְ שְׁמוֹ, הוּא בּוֹרֵא וּמַנְהִיג לְכָל הַבְּרוּאִים, וְהוּא לְבַדּוֹ עָשָׂה, וְעוֹשֶׂה, וְיַעֲשֶׂה לְכָל הַמַּעֲשִׂים:

ב. אֲנִי מַאֲמִין בֶּאֱמוּנָה שְׁלֵמָה, שֶׁהַבּוֹרֵא יִתְבָּרַךְ שְׁמוֹ, הוּא יָחִיד, וְאֵין יְחִידוּת כָּמוֹהוּ בְּשׁוּם פָּנִים, וְהוּא לְבַדּוֹ אֱלֹקֵינוּ הָיָה הֹוֶה וְיִהְיֶה:

ג. אֲנִי מַאֲמִין בֶּאֱמוּנָה שְׁלֵמָה, שֶׁהַבּוֹרֵא יִתְבָּרַךְ שְׁמוֹ, אֵינוֹ גוּף, וְלֹא יַשִּׂיגוּהוּ מַשִּׂיגֵי הַגּוּף, וְאֵין לוֹ שׁוּם דִּמְיוֹן כְּלָל:

ד. אֲנִי מַאֲמִין בֶּאֱמוּנָה שְׁלֵמָה, שֶׁהַבּוֹרֵא יִתְבָּרַךְ שְׁמוֹ, הוּא רִאשׁוֹן וְהוּא אַחֲרוֹן:

ה. אֲנִי מַאֲמִין בֶּאֱמוּנָה שְׁלֵמָה, שֶׁהַבּוֹרֵא יִתְבָּרַךְ שְׁמוֹ, לוֹ לְבַדּוֹ רָאוּי לְהִתְפַּלֵּל, וְאֵין לְזוּלָתוֹ רָאוּי לְהִתְפַּלֵּל:

ו. אֲנִי מַאֲמִין בֶּאֱמוּנָה שְׁלֵמָה, שֶׁכָּל דִּבְרֵי נְבִיאִים אֱמֶת:

ז. אֲנִי מַאֲמִין בֶּאֱמוּנָה שְׁלֵמָה, שֶׁנְּבוּאַת מֹשֶׁה רַבֵּינוּ עָלָיו הַשָּׁלוֹם הָיְתָה אֲמִתִּית, וְשֶׁהוּא הָיָה אָב לַנְּבִיאִים, לַקּוֹדְמִים לְפָנָיו וְלַבָּאִים אַחֲרָיו:

ח. אֲנִי מַאֲמִין בֶּאֱמוּנָה שְׁלֵמָה, שֶׁכָּל הַתּוֹרָה הַמְּצוּיָה עַתָּה בְּיָדֵינוּ, הִיא הַנְּתוּנָה לְמֹשֶׁה רַבֵּינוּ עָלָיו הַשָּׁלוֹם:

ט. אֲנִי מַאֲמִין בֶּאֱמוּנָה שְׁלֵמָה, שֶׁזֹּאת הַתּוֹרָה לֹא תְּהֵא מֻחְלֶפֶת, וְלֹא תְּהֵא תּוֹרָה אַחֶרֶת מֵאֵת הַבּוֹרֵא יִתְבָּרַךְ שְׁמוֹ:

י. אֲנִי מַאֲמִין בֶּאֱמוּנָה שְׁלֵמָה, שֶׁהַבּוֹרֵא יִתְבָּרַךְ שְׁמוֹ, יוֹדֵעַ כָּל מַעֲשֵׂה בְּנֵי אָדָם וְכָל מַחְשְׁבוֹתָם, שֶׁנֶּאֱמַר הַיּוֹצֵר יַחַד לִבָּם, הַמֵּבִין אֶל כָּל מַעֲשֵׂיהֶם:

יא. אֲנִי מַאֲמִין בֶּאֱמוּנָה שְׁלֵמָה, שֶׁהַבּוֹרֵא יִתְבָּרַךְ שְׁמוֹ, גּוֹמֵל טוֹב לְשׁוֹמְרֵי מִצְוֹתָיו, וּמַעֲנִישׁ לְמִי שֶׁיַּעֲבוֹר עַל מִצְוֹתָיו:

יב. אֲנִי מַאֲמִין בֶּאֱמוּנָה שְׁלֵמָה, בְּבִיאַת הַמָּשִׁיחַ, וְאַף עַל פִּי שֶׁיִּתְמַהְמֵהַּ, עִם כָּל זֶה, אֲחַכֶּה לּוֹ בְּכָל יוֹם שֶׁיָּבֹא:

יג. אֲנִי מַאֲמִין בֶּאֱמוּנָה שְׁלֵמָה, שֶׁתִּהְיֶה תְּחִיַּת הַמֵּתִים, בְּעֵת שֶׁתַּעֲלֶה רָצוֹן מֵאֵת הַבּוֹרֵא יִתְבָּרַךְ שְׁמוֹ, וְיִתְעַלֶּה זִכְרוֹ לָעַד, וּלְנֵצַח נְצָחִים:

The 13 Principles

1. "I believe with perfect faith that the Creator is the Creator and Driving Force of all the creatures. He alone made, makes, and will make all happenings."

2. "I believe with perfect faith that the Creator is one. There is no oneness like Him—at all. He alone is our G-d—He was, He is, He will be."

3. "I believe with perfect faith that the Creator is not a body. Physical concepts do not apply to Him. There is nothing comparable to Him at all."

4. "I believe with perfect faith that the Creator is the beginning and the end."

5. "I believe with perfect faith that to the Creator—to Him alone—is it appropriate to pray. It is not appropriate to pray to another."

6. "I believe with perfect faith that all the words of the prophets are true."

7. "I believe with perfect faith that the prophecy of Moshe (Moses) our teacher was absolutely true. He was the father of all prophets, those who came before him and those who came after him."

8. "I believe with perfect faith that the Torah which we have today in our hands is the actual Torah given to Moshe our teacher."

9. "I believe with perfect faith that the Torah will not be changed and there will never be any other Torah given by the Creator."

10. "I believe with perfect faith that the Creator knows all the deeds and all the thoughts of every human being, as it is written, *He has fashioned every heart; He pays attention to all their deeds.*"

11. "I believe with perfect faith that the Creator rewards those who keep His commandments, and punishes those who violate His commandments."

12. "I believe with perfect faith in the coming of the Messiah, and though he may tarry—nevertheless I wait for him each day."

13. "I believe with perfect faith that the dead will be brought back to life when the Creator wills it, and His memory will be elevated for ever and ever."

Note To The Reader

This book has been specially designed to make regular review of its ideas easy and enjoyable. Thus, as you will notice, the running text is supplemented with numerous footnotes, many of which significantly deepen the ideas touched upon in the main body. As footnotes, however, they can more or less be skipped if the reader prefers to read the entire book (or a particular chapter) relatively quickly. Conversely, a reader who wants a deeper, more satisfying understanding the first time around should find the footnotes, especially the lengthier ones, indispensable. In either case, this book is designed to be read and reread regularly. Use the format to suit your style.

Overview Of The Thirteen Principles

CHAPTER 1

The Thirteen Principles

In his commentary on the Mishnah,[1] the Rambam (Maimonides) described the Thirteen Principles of Faith. Later, the Thirteen Principles were capsulized and formulated into the well-known wording found in the *siddur*: *Ani ma'amim b'emunah shlaima* . . . ("I believe with perfect faith . . .") Both the concept of the Thirteen Principles and its wording hold a central place in Judaism. As such, every conscientious Jew must endeavor to make them a central part of his or her life. Let us begin doing so by analyzing the concepts and wording very carefully.

The first question is, what did the Rambam find in these principles which distinguish them from other Torah concepts? Indeed, are there any concepts in the Torah which are not vital? Imagine a person hired to find the solution to a very perplexing mathematical problem. Pages and pages of calculations and formulas must be

---

[1] Sanhedrin, *Perek Chelek*.

written in order to end up with the final tabulation. For the sake of illustration, let's say the person has to take into consideration over one million numbers to arrive at the final tally. Can he afford to make a mistake with one number? Which number is more important, more fundamental? None. If one number is off the final tally will be off.

Torah, from beginning to end, is one answer. Thus, "... if someone denies the authenticity of even the tiniest point of a *yud*, it is as if he denies the entire Torah." If every point of every letter in the Torah is vital, then certainly every letter is vital. If every letter is vital, then certainly every word is vital. And if every word is vital, then unquestionably every concept is vital. Why then does the Rambam enumerate only thirteen concepts as the "Principles" of Faith? Every component of Torah is vital!

The answer is that a mistake made in any other part of the Torah is a mistake with limited repercussions. It is a "local" mistake; a mistake which does not necessarily effect anything else. However, if you made a mistake in one of the Thirteen Principles it is not just a local, isolated mistake. It is a mistake with global ramifications for your spiritual well-being; a mistake that perforce breeds many other mistakes. A deficiency in any other Torah law or concept is like having a non-functioning limb. A deficiency in the Thirteen Principles is like having a malfunctioning or non-functioning brain.

According to the Rambam, then, the Thirteen Principles are the roots of faith upon which the tree of Torah is

The Thirteen Principles

anchored and nourished. If the roots are unhealthy, the entire tree is in danger. If the roots are healthy, the tree is not only healthy but capable of withstanding high winds and decimating forces which might otherwise topple it.[1] *Consequently, a given individual's experience and appreciation of life, with all its highs and lows, is directly dependent upon how well that individual incorporates the Thirteen Principles into his or her mindset.*

That is the first point to understand. Each of the Thirteen Principles is a life-line; a vital life-force of spiritual nourishment upon which happiness and success depend. Before shifting our attention to them, though, let us turn to the opening formula with which those Principles are worded.

---

[1] Consider the metaphor of the rooted tree we employed in *Choose Life!*:

> Life is a continuous flow of ever-changing, surging currents. Fads, philosophies, finances, leaders and governments are in constant flux. Nothing in this world has permanence. The success with which we meet change and adversity is dependent on how true and well-rooted our beliefs are.
> The wisest of all men called Torah "... a tree of life to those who grab hold of her" (Proverbs 3:18). That tree is the inner truth of life, which does not change. It stands in the middle while the waters of the modern, mundane world rush all about. There are other things in the water which may at first appear to be able to save us from drowning, but when we grab onto them in our moment of need we find out that they were nothing other than dead wood or shallowly rooted trees.
> No outlook in the long record of mankind has weathered the ebb and flow of history like Torah. It is not just another philosophy, psychology or self-help trend, and it is not just another religion. It is the root of this world, and what you gain by grabbing onto it is not just some transient happiness—you gain life, real life.

Beyond Survival

I Believe

What does it mean to say, "I believe"? Is it a sign of intellectual weakness? Or is there a deeper understanding implied in such an admission?

In order to fully understand anything in the physical world we must utilize all five senses. The more senses we employ, the more we understand. Take an ordinary table, for example. We can see its color, feel its texture, hear its sturdiness (by knocking on it), etc. If we are missing any one of those senses we do not fully know what it is.

Consider a person born blind. No matter how much we tell him about color, aesthetics, etc., he will not perceive what we perceive. True, the blind person has an imagination. He has his own impressions about the world. He can touch a table, get its dimensions, find out what it is made of, but no matter how much he knows he will have an entirely different picture of the table than a person with sight.[1] Now, consider what happens if we could implement a new medical technique which would give sight to such a person. His entire world—the only world he knew, loved, and appreciated—falls away instantly. Whatever he had imagined the world to be, the reality of what it is changes everything drastically and immediately.

---

[1] Or consider the world of a deaf person. Picture him at a symphony. What will he think of the conductor jumping around like a maniac, the musicians periodically puffing their cheeks, etc.? How will he interpret the experience of a symphony? He can imagine what it is like, but his imagination will vary greatly from those who possess the faculty of hearing.

The Thirteen Principles

If one sense is missing our entire world changes—and changes drastically. Each of us has his own perceptions of the world, and as real as we think them to be they are only as real as the number (and quality) of senses we use to form our perceptions. Should any one of our senses be missing or deficient our entire world view can be devastatingly wrong.

Most of us are unaware that there exists a vital sense organ beyond the five senses. The sixth sense is an uncanny ability to see things which a person using only logic and reason cannot perceive. In its most highly developed form it manifests itself as telepathy, precognition, or other so-called psychic abilities. Most people probably experience their sixth sense in an especially heightened way at least once in their life. Moreover, some people are very gifted and demonstrate the existence of their sixth sense regularly. A person so endowed has an entirely different perception of the world. His world transcends the five senses.[1]

However, even those who possess an active and authentic sixth sense are not necessarily in possession of their full potential because *there exists an even higher sense than the sixth sense.* To prove it, consider Uri Geller, the famous psychic who impressed people internationally

---

[1] The Modzitzer Rebbe composed one of his most intricately beautiful *niggunim* (songs) while undergoing surgery *without* anesthesia. His connection to the world of song, a realm totally beyond the five senses, helped him block out the pain his senses were experiencing. Such a person, exploiting his sixth sense, lives on the same planet, but experiences a vastly different world than people depending merely on the five senses.

Beyond Survival

with his ability to bend metal spoons using only his mind. His exploits were recorded on film in front of doubting eye-witnesses. Apparently, he possessed an authentic spiritual, sixth sense power. However, does that mean he was connected to the truth? Tarzan could bend metal with his physical strength; Uri Geller could do so with his spiritual muscles. It is an impressive feat, but is his apparent psychic strength proof that everything he says is true? Obviously, such psychic prowess is an ability independent of truth. Spirituality is something beyond the five senses, *but not all spirituality necessarily emanates from the realm of truth*. It can originate from numerous other sources, including the realm of *tumah* (defilement), a realm totally independent of the realm of truth.[1]

There is a "seventh" sense, however. And this sense is the highest of all. Moreover, it is attainable by all. One need not have the sixth sense or even the five senses as a prerequisite. The seventh sense is our instinct for truth.

". . . He has set the world in their heart . . . ."[2] All of us have an instinct, an intuition, for the truth. Each of us is in possession of a picture of the world as it ideally should be.[3] That intuitive picture of true reality may be buried

---

[1] Thus, Abraham gave the sons of his concubine "the name of *tumah*," i.e. spiritual-mystical sciences not intrinsically connected to truth, to G–d. (*Sanhedrin* 91a)

[2] Ecclesiastes (*Koheles*) 3:11.

[3] Thus, the Sages teach that a fetus "sees from one end of the world to the other" and is taught the entire Torah while still in the womb (*Niddah* 30b). In other words, it perceives ultimate reality. At birth, however, an angel touches the fetus on the lip, and thereby causes it

The Thirteen Principles

somewhere deep inside, but it beats in each heart nonetheless. At the same time, however, it must be admitted that not all intuitions are true. Our eyes can see hallucinations; our ears can hear make-believe sounds; even a genuine psychic's sixth sense can prove misleading. And if our physical senses can be deceived, what can be said in defense of our intellectual sense of the world, a sense which develops from impressions dependent upon upbringing, opinion, and assumption? When the entire complex of human motivations and subtle, hidden affections are taken into consideration it becomes clear that what we intuit (or think we intuit) may not be true at all. We are all very good at fooling ourselves and our natural intuitive sense may very well be corrupted. Ultimate truth, therefore, cannot only come from within. If we are to know the truth at all, there must be an outside standard to which it measures up.

In the realm of the five senses that outside standard is called science (at least in its ideal form). In the realm of the sixth sense, it is the science of mysticism (which is, essentially, the science of the spiritual realm). In the realm of Truth, there is an outside standard as well. It is Torah.[1]

---

to lose its panoramic understanding. Nevertheless, an impression, however faint, remains. That impression, it can be said, serves as the source of the intuition for truth each adult possesses.

[1] Of course, science and mysticism ultimately have their roots in Torah as well. And without Torah even the scientist's science is not science. Thus, for instance, the 19th century scientist who subscribed to the Static Universe Theory (that the physical universe always existed) was disconnected from the truth stated in the Torah that the

Beyond Survival

Truth is only with G–d.[1] What G–d does not tell us is not real. And thus G–d made a special point to bequeath absolute, objective Truth to humanity by giving the Jewish People the Torah on Mount Sinai. Absolute, objective Truth in this world exists only in the Torah. Without Torah, we are like the blind man who can only imagine what the world looks like.

The question is, what is the "organ" of truth? Eyes are the organs of sight; ears of hearing; skin of touch; the nose of smell; the tongue of taste. They serve as vehicles for our perception of the physical world. Similarly, the soul is the "organ" of spiritual inspiration. It helps us perceive the mystical-psychic side of life. However, how does one perceive the deep truth underlying the world? What faculty do we have to see it?

The answer is *emunah*—faith or belief.

Emunah is an organ of expression in the sense that it filters our experience. All experience is shaped by

---

universe had a beginning. "Discoveries" in the 20th century scientific world confirm the Torah's assertion. And that serves as a paradigm for all other truths. There is no such thing as true science or mysticism if it is not rooted in the "Torah of Truth."

[1] The Sages praise any judge who can judge ". . . a case to its absolute truth (*emes l'amito*, literally, truth to its truth)." Why is the emphasis on "absolute" (i.e. the double truth)? Simple truth is truth ascertained with the tools of intellect. "Absolute truth," on the other hand, is the truth which comes from above, and the only tool to ascertain such truth is *emunah*. That is why the Sages conclude that a judge who judges a case to its absolute truth "becomes a partner with G–d in the work of creation." By rendering a judgment which transcends mere man-deduced truth he has brought absolute truth, i.e. an aspect of G–d Himself, down into the world. Such a person is rightly described as a partner with G–d in the work of creation.

The Thirteen Principles

attitudes. If one is arrogant, one will be close-minded to anything which threatens the ego. *Emunah*, on the other hand, is an attitude which predisposes one toward experiencing truth. It is expressed in traits such as honesty and humility because a believer is someone who first and foremost humbly recognizes that he is a hopelessly subjective creature. He realizes that he is in the blind. Just as the blind man can only imagine what the physical world looks like, so, too, the finite human being—even the most brilliant, scholarly one—only imagines reality. Thus, the admission that one is by definition a creature of faith is the beginning of wisdom because it is the most honest appraisal of one's situation. If we think we can know truth through our own five senses or even through our soul's sixth sense we are fooling ourselves.

Thus, "I believe . . ." is a higher declaration than "I know . . . ." One who says "I know . . ." reveals his limitations. He is admitting that the statement about to leave his lips is nothing more than his perception of what *he thinks* he knows to be true. On the other hand, one who introduces his thought by saying "I believe . . ." displays his *knowledge* that his senses are deceiving, that he is blind, that what he perceives to be true is only his imagination of what the truth is. Thus, the moment I say, "I know . . ." (i.e. that I am the arbiter of true knowledge), I am admitting (despite my denial of it) that I am in the dark.[1]

---

[1] Scientists are notorious for making statements such as, "We *know* such and such to be true." However, a few years later a new discovery

Beyond Survival

In summary, then, there is a two-step process. First, we have to humbly admit we are blind. Without that admission we are incapable of coming to the Truth as it really exists, *as G–d knows it.* Only after recognizing that *we are by definition creatures of faith,* are we ready for step two: Torah.

And, by the way, that is why the seventh sense, *emunah*, corresponds to the seventh day, *Shabbos*.[1] On *Shabbos* we are helpless. If the telephone rings we cannot pick it up. If there is distant place we want to visit we cannot

---

is made and the next generation's scientist will say, "They (he does not include himself with the earlier researchers) used to *believe* such and such. Now we *know* . . ." Little does the next generation's scientist realize that in all likelihood future research will likewise undermine his knowledge and thereby expose it as belief. Yet, he will rarely say, "We believe such and such to be true." Belief is a word that is taboo for many scientists, even though it is not only a sign of humility but the only true way to formulate one's findings.

To further emphasize the point, it is well known in scholarly circles that a discovery in the early part of this century places all science on a foundation of questionable sturdiness. In 1931, mathematician Kurt Godel demonstrated that at the deepest level all mathematics is based on axioms, i.e. statements that cannot be proved true. Since scientific proofs invariably rest on the power of mathematics, Godel's discovery means that even the foundations of the physical sciences are fundamentally flawed; even the best theories potentially rest ". . . on sand" (John Barrow, a famous English astronomer, cited in *Newsweek*, November 30, 1992). The point is not to undermine the potential value of science, but to expose the arrogance of those who say they "know" when in fact the best they can say is they "believe."

[1] The first five days correspond to the five senses. During those five days only elements of the physical world were created. The sixth day, however, corresponds to the sixth sense. On the sixth day G–d blew the eternal soul into a creature of the planet. (See Chapter 2, *Oneness And The Soul.*) The seventh day, though, is highest of all and corresponds to the Sabbath, as we now shall explain.

The Thirteen Principles

drive the car. We cannot turn on or off lights. We are powerless to fulfill our needs the way we are used to fulfilling them. However, in our very disconnection from the power sources of our work-a-day week we connect to a Higher Power. *Shabbos* gives us pause to think about true reality. Is this world real? For six days I was working and running around. Was that the real me? Am I my job, my career, my connections, my position in the weekday world? *Shabbos* reminds me of the truth of my existence through my *withdrawal* from the world of illusion. We let G–d run the show on *Shabbos*. That requires faith. That type of faith, though, is the bedrock of knowledge.

Knowledge is important; in fact, it is as vitally important as faith—but only when emanating from Torah. With Torah a person can say, "I know" (if indeed the knowledge he is about to express emanates from the Torah). However, the prerequisite for Torah is *emunah* (faith, belief). *Emunah* is the awareness that if there is truth in the world it only can be in conjunction with G–d, with G–d's knowledge. Thus, "I believe . . ." is the most foundational affirmation of Truth. It exceeds "I know . . ." (said independently of Torah), and therefore is the beginning of the Thirteen Principles.

Perfect Faith

"I believe with perfect faith . . . ." What is "perfect" faith (literally, faith that is "complete," *emunah*

Beyond Survival

"*shlaima*")? What extra level does "perfect" faith include which faith alone does not?

In order to answer that question we must ask the following: Is Judaism based on belief or knowledge? More to the point: Everything the Torah tells us about leaving Egypt—are we expected to believe it is true or to know it is true?

The fact is that Judaism is a belief based on knowledge. I was told by people, who in turn were told by other people, who in turn were told by other people, and so on uninterruptedly, stretching back to those people who were there. Since I was told by people it is essentially something I believe. However, since there is no way the people who experienced the original events could have been mistaken my belief is based on knowledge.

How do we know that the people who experienced the founding events of the Jewish Nation could not have been mistaken? For one thing, those events did not happen to one person, but to an entire nation. And it was not just one event, but many events over a period of time. And it did not just happen in an isolated part of the world, but in the middle of arguably history's most famous civilization. Furthermore, the documentation includes the names of the people involved, their family genealogies, their dates and places of birth, their travels, etc. It even includes information about the Egyptians, their names, the places they occupied, the idols they served, the unusual details of their downfall[1]—all of

---

[1] Among the most noteworthy of archaeological evidences support-

The Thirteen Principles

which is so accurate that archaeologists today use the Torah as the basis for their excavations.[1]

Other religions admit that their ideas are based exclusively on belief.[2] One person claimed to have received a revelation or performed a miracle. Torah is based on knowledge, however. Not one of the original Jews had to

---

ing the Torah's account of the downfall of Egypt is the Ipuwer Papyrus (which historians have dated around the time of the story of the exodus). Ipuwer was an ancient Egyptian who wrote how his land was devastated by a series of disasters resembling the Torah's account, including the river turning to blood ("The river is blood . . . Plague is throughout the land, blood is everywhere. Men shrink from tasting . . . and thirst after water."), pestilence ("All animals, their hearts weep, cattle moan, smitten with pestilence."), famine, ("No fruit, nor herbs are found . . . Grain has perished on every side."), death ("He who places his brother in the ground is everywhere . . . It is groaning that is throughout the land mingled with lamentations.").

Historians also admit that the downfall of Egypt is essentially a mystery. In fact, Jewish history after the exodus continues for at least 500 years detailing war after war with every neighboring power, except for the very noticeable absence of Egypt. What happened to the region's most dominant empire? Even the secular historians have no satisfactory answer (other than admitting to the validity of the Torah's account, which they do not do for that would be sacrilege to them).

[1] "Science is now in a position to state categorically that the Bible is factual till proven otherwise." Will Durant, in *Story of Civilization*, Volume 1; see our discussion on Principle 8.

[2] The beginnings Islam and Christianity, for instance, are restricted to the more or less private happenings of at best a few individuals. These individuals then went about convincing others to "believe" in their experience or revelation. Knowing they could never claim as impressive a claim to Divine intervention as the redemption from Egypt or the revelation at Sinai, they therefore came to base their religions on our Torah and its unique claims. (Christianity and Islam view themselves as heirs to Judaism, not brand new religions per say.) As for the particular events which distinguished their beginnings, however, they relied on winning others over to their conviction.

rely on someone else's revelation. Everyone experienced the ten plagues. Everyone walked through the parted Sea. Everyone heard G–d's voice on Sinai. Everyone ate manna for forty years in the desert. That is knowledge. "You have been *shown* to know that G–d is the [only] G–d . . . ."[1] Torah is based on events that everyone was shown first hand. That is a foundation of knowledge.

Judaism, then, is the dynamic between faith and knowledge. I know that G–d exists, that He took us out of Egypt, that the Torah is true—because there was no way to deny the experience of my nation's original generation. What do I believe? Whatever the Torah says.[2] If the Torah says that lighting a fire on *Shabbos* is something which destroys worlds, then I believe that to be true even though I myself cannot see those worlds getting destroyed. Or, for instance, if the Torah says that

---

[1] Deut. 4:35.
[2] In another sense, our faith in Torah is not only historically based, but rationally based as well. Torah is the logical extension of the idea that the Creator is a personal G–d. (The idea, by the way, that G–d is not merely a Creator who created the world long ago, but a G–d who is intimately involved with each individual even now is the import of the opening to the Ten Commandments where G–d introduces Himself as the G–d who freed the Jews from Egypt, not the G–d who created the world. The latter statement might be used to claim that G–d created the world and then disassociated Himself from it [as is indeed the claim of many ancient philosophers and present-day Deists]. The actual revelation, however, made clear that G–d was still involved with creation, as evidenced by His miraculous intervention against Egypt on behalf of the Jewish People.). Once I *know* G–d is the type of G–d who is personally involved with my life and everyone's life, it follows that He would give me guidance and "instructions" (Torah means "instruction") on how to live my life. And what more impressive "instruction" booklet is there than Torah?

The Thirteen Principles

the Jewish People are eternal, then I believe that the Jewish People are eternal. I admit that eternity has to do with the future, which is something I can only believe in. Nevertheless, it is a belief based on knowledge. G-d said in the Torah that we are eternal.[1] Therefore, even if it strikes me as logical to say that the Jewish People are eternal (after all, even historians are baffled how they have survived to this day[2]), nevertheless, it is greater to say, "I believe with perfect faith" that the Jewish People are eternal because greater than intellectual knowledge is the fact that it says so in the Torah—the Torah which G-d gave to my ancestors when He took them out of Egypt. Their experience was undeniable. Therefore, my faith is whole when I link it to knowledge; when I express it in terms of the authority vested in the Torah. That is perfect faith, a faith founded on knowledge.

In conclusion, then, although we possess beliefs, our faith is based on knowledge. And that is what is referred to by "perfect" faith. Perfect faith—whole, complete faith—is the combination of faith and knowledge. Every belief goes back to the root, which is the knowledge that G-d is the "G-d who took us out of the land of Egypt, out of the house of bondage."[3]

---

[1] Although the eternity of the Jewish People is stated or alluded to in many places, in my opinion the strongest statement is: "You are children to G-d your G-d." A child is the extension of the parent. If G-d is eternal, then His child is eternal.
[2] "What is the secret of his [the Jews'] immortality?"—Mark Twain, "Concerning the Jews," Harper's Magazine, 1899. (See *Choose Life!*, pages 105-106, where we have brought the full quote.)
[3] As we have now explained the matter, a seeming contradiction be-

Beyond Survival

Knowledge Today

A legitimate question is, can we *know* this today? Yes, our belief rests on a solid foundation of knowledge. But, still, wouldn't it be better to have knowledge founded upon knowledge? Can we *know* it ourselves today?

To answer that, let us ask a question. Which is stronger, seeing or perceiving? Is seeing something with our eyes better evidence of reality or is understanding it with our mind greater proof? The answer is that in some ways understanding with our mind is stronger. Let me elaborate.

Today, only fifty years after the holocaust, there are people who claim that the holocaust never took place. There is already a now famous story about one revisionist

---

tween two different writings of the Rambam, one in the *Mishnah Torah* and the other in his *Sefer HaMitzvos*, is resolved. In the *Mishnah Torah*, he writes: "The foundation of all foundations, and the pillar of all knowledge is to *know* there is a G–d." How does one know that? The Rambam continues: "Because it says, *I am the G–d who took you out of Egypt, out of the house of bondage.*" G–d does not introduce Himself as the G–d who created the universe. Since no human being was there to witness the creation, that would have required faith. However, the G–d who performed all the miracles in Egypt was a G–d they had seen with their own eyes. He was "knowledge" to them. That is why the Rambam emphasizes that it is a *mitzvah* to "know" there is a G–d. However, in *Sefer HaMitzvos* the Rambam writes: "It is a commandment to *believe* in G–d, because it says, *I am the G–d who took you out of Egypt, out of the house of bondage.*" Here he says it is a commandment to "believe," not to "know." The resolution is that it is a commandment to both know and believe. Our belief must be based on knowledge, as we have said, and the two different wordings in the Rambam's writings reflect that. (For more on the relationship between faith and knowledge, see *Darkness Before Dawn*, Chapter 3, and *Self-Esteem*, the essay on *Pesach*.)

The Thirteen Principles

group in Los Angeles which distributed flyers and propaganda that the entire holocaust was a hoax created by the Jews. The leader of the group paid for an advertisement in the paper challenging anyone to prove the validity of the fact that six million Jews were murdered in concentration camps. And he offered a $50,000 reward for anyone who could prove it.

A holocaust survivor approached him and showed him a number tattooed on his arm.

"You made the tattoo yourself," he told him.

"But I went through the holocaust. I saw it with my own eyes," he responded.

"Why should we believe you? What is the absolute proof?"

The survivor argued, but in futility. The anti-Semite never intended to accept any arguments. Ultimately, though, the survivor brought his case to court. The $50,000 was obviously not the main issue. The main issue was refuting the revisionists. The outcome of the trial depended upon the survivor bringing proof that the Nazis indeed perpetrated the holocaust.

"What is your proof?"

"The crematoriums in Auschwitz still stand."

"That's just a museum. It doesn't prove anything."

"What about all the documented films of speeches, marches, and the camps in action?"

"The same people who could make up a museum made up the films. Hollywood does it all the time."

Beyond Survival

"What about all the papers on file documenting the Nazis' plans?"

"Forgeries and fabrications."

Every item that was obvious to the eye was refuted as fiction. Eyes can be deceived. Filmmakers can produce movies. Experts can forge documents, etc.

The case was ultimately won when the survivor's lawyers lined up fifty eye-witnesses who were thoroughly cross-examined and whose stories were scrutinized for any inconsistencies. Only after their experiences proved consistent did the judge conclude they had proven the holocaust beyond doubt. The point is that movies, books, museums, et al., would not prove it. Eyes can be deceived. Only eye-witness testimony established the fact in the court's eyes.

That case and other similar incidents caused people to think. Holocaust survivors in particular wanted to find a way to guarantee that the memory of the event would not be erased or denied after they passed on. One group of survivors decided to shoulder the responsibility of ensuring the memory of the holocaust. They set up their own guidelines toward that end. Let us for a moment put ourselves in their shoes and imagine how we might guarantee that the holocaust will never be denied.

First, we would want to collect as many eye-witness stories as possible, and we would want as large a collection as possible. Not everyone's story would be automatically accepted, though. Only stories from members of the group would be authoritative. To become a member, one

The Thirteen Principles

would have to have been there himself. Furthermore, he would have to possess and be willing to display some physical sign commemorating his ordeal, such as the numbered tattoo on his body, or the wearing of a distinctive piece of clothing (such as the yellow star), or the display of something unique in his house. Next, after collecting the stories we might edit them all into one manuscript, which would be the single authorized, authentic account of those who witnessed the holocaust first hand. Moreover, every member would be obligated to have in his possession at least one copy of the authoritative manuscript, which he would be expected to read daily and finish in its entirety yearly. It would also be a good idea to set aside a definite time one day a week, every week, to read the manuscript publicly, not hesitating to correct any mispronunciations or misunderstandings. And, most importantly, it would be vital to stress to the next generation how crucial it would be to faithfully continue the group's practices in order to ensure that the information would never be forgotten.

Let us now take the scenario one step further and imagine the scene 200 years hence when another group of anti-Semites offer a large sum of money to anyone who can prove the holocaust happened. The case comes to court and all the old newsreels are dismissed, just as they were in the Los Angeles case. Finally, the leader of the survivors' group says, "Your honor, 200 years ago our forefathers set up a club of holocaust survivors, and we, their descendants, have instituted many unique ideas into

Beyond Survival

our lives on the basis of those original survivors' wishes. Today the club numbers fifteen million. We have been copying and reading and teaching to our children the original authorized manuscript for 200 years. No two copies differ. And we have all these traditions—tatoos on our flesh, distinct clothes, special testimonials in our houses, etc.—which we have been keeping just to memorialize the events that really happened to our great-great grandparents." And so on.

That type of testimony would prove quite powerful. A movie or document could be fabricated, but millions of people centering their lives around testimonies which all commemorate a single, momentous (albeit infamous) event requires a coordination, perseverance, and commitment that negates the possibility of fabrication.

That is Jewish tradition.

We have a special holiday, Passover, where we go to great lengths and expense to commemorate the single, momentous, original event which marked the beginning of our peoplehood. We have a Torah, hand-written today as it was first put down millennia ago, which is the authorized account of that event. In addition, we set aside one day every week to discuss the "authorized manuscript" and sanctify that day "in remembrance of the exodus from Egypt." We put *tefillin* on our bodies and *mezuzos* on our houses, each containing parchments reminding us of the original exodus. And not one Torah scroll, *tefillin* scroll, or *mezuzah* differs from another. No matter where Jews are or ever were the words are exactly

The Thirteen Principles

the same. We have tradition after tradition designed exclusively to memorialize the events that happened to one original generation of Jews long ago, events which were shown them "... to know that G–d is the G–d in heaven; there is no other."

The survival of these traditions is in some ways even greater proof than the events themselves. Is there a greater miracle than the little *mezuzah*? Jews have been scattered across the globe more than 2,000 years. Yet, the Yemenite Jew, the Pakistani Jew, the Hungarian Jew, the Russian Jew, the American Jew—all have the same *mezuzah*. And for just one *mezuzah* to be in compliance with Jewish law close to 5,000 highly detailed laws must be observed! *Tefillin* must conform to approximately 30,000 laws! And a Torah scroll must be in conformity to well over one million laws!

Furthermore, consider the way Jews commemorate the historical exodus from Egypt. The customs with which each family conducts its own *seder* on Passover night is more varied than one can imagine. I am one of nine children, and I can assure you that though I and my brothers try to imitate the way our father conducted his *seder* we each conduct it in our own unique way. Similarly, each of my sons has his own unique style. And if that is true for just one family, how diverse must be the *seder* nights of others families. And if that diversity exists within families rooted in the customs of Europe, how much more diverse the mixture of customs must be when one includes those of the Yemenite or Pakistani Jew. Yet,

Beyond Survival

despite all of these variations, *each Jew tells the exact same story without deviation!* The same four cups, the same ten plagues, the same *matzah*, the same *afikomen*—each individual and each group center their Passover night *seder* on the same story, the same event!

Is there a greater miracle? Is there greater evidence that there was one original event from which everything else sprang? If not for the strength of the original tradition, there is no doubt that 2,000 years of isolation, persecution, and decimation of numbers would have created deviation in the core event.[1]

My point is that so much of our tradition is founded upon the idea that momentous events happened to us in Egypt long ago that today we too can say we have knowledge of the original events. True, we did not experience those events like those who were there bodily, but they did not have more than 3,300 years of living a lifestyle which commemorates the original events. They saw it with their eyes, but, on the other hand, our traditions supply so much testimony concerning the original Jewish historical experience that they constitute a type of revelation themselves. That revelation exists right there in our *mezuzos, tefillin,* Torah scrolls, holy days, and other traditions.

---

[1] Furthermore, do not forget that the Torah predicted the isolation, persecution, and decimation beforehand, (for instance [Deut. 4:27], "And G–d will scatter you among the nations, and you shall remain few in number...") and yet promised that the words of Torah will never be forgotten from Jewish descendants (Isaiah 59:20-21).

The Thirteen Principles

Thus, we can "know" today that the Torah is absolutely true—not simply because our fathers told us, but because we possess the knowledge. We possess numerous testimonies which appeal to the mind. With a little reflection upon those testimonies, the absolute truth of Torah becomes as obvious today as ever, perhaps even more obvious than even to those who merely witnessed the events with their eyes.

Summary

Ani ma'amim: "I believe..." that human senses are inadequate to comprehend true reality. I can only begin to hope to discover the truth when I first admit how in the dark I am; how much I am a creature of faith. Even a man-made body of knowledge purporting to reach the absolute Truth is by definition limited (since it is man-made). Only a body of knowledge *as G–d knows it* can be true.

B'emunah shlaima: "... with faith that is complete...." My faith is "perfect" or "complete" when I realize that the Torah is the Truth *as G–d knows it*, because it backs up its claim to being truth with nothing less than the exodus from Egypt (the plagues, the revelation, etc.), a once-in-history exhibition of G–d's power and will designed to show my ancestors in an undeniable way that the lifestyle and values laid forth in His Torah were absolutely true. Moreover, many factors today—including the survival of numerous highly accurate and consistent traditions all pointing to the extraordinary original experience of the exodus—further fortify my conviction and make my faith complete.

Chapter 2

The Creator

CHAPTER 2

The Creator

Principle 1: "I believe with perfect faith that the Creator, blessed be His name, is the Creator and Driving Force of all the creatures. He alone made, makes, and will make all happenings."

In this and several of the other Principles we address G–d as the Creator. Why do we call Him Creator? Isn't it an insult? After all, He is much more than a Creator.

To illustrate, imagine I made a table. Would it not be a limitation to call me "the table-maker"? I am more than a person who made a table. Now, if labeling me a table-maker is an insult to my stature, then to be called the Creator, even of the entire universe, is an infinitely greater insult to G–d. A human being more closely resembles a table than G–d resembles His creation. Why then do we call Him Creator?

The Sages teach that every element of creation sings praises to G–d. The sun, earth, wind, animal kingdom, fish kingdom, vegetable kingdom, etc.—all sing praises to their Creator. However, none of that is really praise of G–d, because the acknowledgment of G–d by the physical world is itself a product of G–d's doing. He designed them to do His will and to praise Him.

Human beings, on the other hand, have been given freedom to choose to deny G–d. "I did it myself," we can say—or at least deceive ourselves into saying. Since we are the only ones capable of this self-delusion, we are also the only creations capable of *choosing* to acknowledge G–d's dominance in our lives. The rest of creation has no choice but to acknowledge this fact. When we sing praises to G–d, declaring that we exist only because He created us, we praise G–d in a way nothing else possibly can.

And that is why we address G–d here as Creator. By calling Him "Creator" we do not presume to define His essence, but rather we acknowledge and express our relationship to Him as His creations, an acknowledgment no other creation is capable of rendering.

This Moment

There are three stances a believer can have. The first is simple monotheism, the belief that there is a G–d who created the world, which is represented by the name *Elokim*. *Elokim* is the name used during the creation of the first six days. Its numerical value is equivalent to the numerical value of the Hebrew word for "nature,"[1]

The Creator

suggesting that *Elokim* refers to the G–d who set up the natural laws of the universe. In theory, the power inherent in *Elokim* alone would have been enough to create the world and to let it run on its own according to the natural laws. At the minimum, all human beings, according to the Torah, are obligated to believe in *Elokim*.

The second level of belief is that which G–d revealed to our forefathers, represented by the name *Sha–dai*. *Sha–dai* means "enough," which the Maharal[2] explains to mean that G–d supplies the world with just "enough" sustenance for it to run—not too much and not too little. *Sha–dai*, then, is the level where one recognizes that not only is G–d the Creator of a perfectly conceived mechanical universe, but that He also intervenes now and then whenever He wills. Our forefathers saw that G–d could overturn the rules of nature as He pleased.

The third level is that revealed to Moshe, as represented by the name *Havaya*,[3] i.e. the four-letter Tetragrammaton, which is a combination of the Hebrew words "is, was, and will be." This level of belief is expressed in the words, "He alone made, makes, and will make all happenings." *Havaya* indicates that G–d is perpetually invigorating the world. He did not just create it once long ago, but each and every moment exists only

---

[1] *Hateva*, literally "the nature," in numerical terms equals eighty-six, the numerical value of *Elokim*.
[2] *Gevuros Hashem* 31.
[3] See Exodus 6:2,3. See our discussion in *Darkness Before Dawn*, Chapter 7, subchapter, "Conclusion;" and *Self-Esteem*, essay on *Pesach*, subchapter, "The Self-Replicating Program."

because He wills it to exist at that very moment.[1] G–d is literally our "respirator." We are dependent upon Him even for our every breath. The heart that pumps, the lungs that breathe, the microscopic molecules that reproduce themselves, the atomic particles that are in constant motion—all are driven continually by G–d. Should He stop driving them for a moment they (and we) would cease to exist. That is why in addition to Creator we call G–d *manhig*, or "Driving Force," which means that G–d is perpetually involved with creation, driving it, running it, even leading it to its destiny.

It is one thing to believe, as does the simple monotheist who acknowledges *Elokim*, that G–d created the world, but it is an entirely different matter to believe He is involved in every happening in the world every second it exists (as implied by *Havaya*). The former view is mechanistic. G–d established the world during the original creation and lets it run on its own according to set rules He founded long ago, at the beginning. The Creator created creation and afterward let nature take its course. At the minimum every human being is obligated to believe that.[2]

---

[1] And that is the import of the words we say every morning, "And in His goodness He renews daily, perpetually (*mechadash b'chall yom tamid*), the work of creation."

[2] *Elokim* is the level Noah recognized, especially after he left the ark and saw a world reborn. It was clearer to him then than ever before that G–d created the world. Similarly, the next level of perception, *Sha–dai*, was obtained by the forefathers, who lived in the aftermath of the Tower of Babel. The lesson of the Tower was that G–d could intervene on the affairs of humanity at will, disrupting what He

The Creator

The demand of belief expressed in this first Principle goes further, though. A light bulb shines. What produces the light? Electricity flowing through the filament. Does the light shine now because a few minutes ago someone flicked the switch? No. It needs an ongoing supply of electricity in order to keep the light shining. Stop that electricity for a moment and the light stops.

The world is the same way. The true reality of the world is that nothing exists outside G–d. G–d is the only true existence. Images on a movie screen do not exist independently. They are nothing more than a combination of a light projector and film. The person on the screen is not a person. It is light in the image of a person. It has no reality by itself. Turn off the projector for one second and the image completely disappears.

So, too, if G–d should cease His "flow of electricity" into us—if He should turn off the projection of His light—for even one instant we will cease to exist. We are not here because G–d gave us intrinsic existence many

---

pleased and perpetuating what He pleased. The highest perception of G–d, however, *Havaya*, was only first revealed through the demise of Egypt. The miraculous manner in which the plagues, the splitting of the sea, and the giving of the Torah were carried out proved that not only does G–d intervene in mankind's affairs, but that there is no such thing as an act which is not G–d's will. *Havaya* is the verb of being—all life is G–d's being, animated.

Thus, Noah, i.e. one who perceives *Elokim*, corresponds to the person who refutes atheism. The forefathers (*Sha–dai* perception) correspond to the one who refutes the idea of an impersonal G–d, i.e. a G–d uninvolved with humanity. Moshe and his generation (*Havaya* perception) correspond to the person who refutes coincidence, i.e. one who recognizes that not even the smallest act lacks G–d's participation or presence.

years ago. You are here now—this moment, as you read these very words—because He wants you to exist even now. We are all part of this moment. This moment exists only because He wills it now.

"He alone made, makes, and will make all happenings." All happenings happen because He presently wants them to happen. That is the essence of this first principle of belief.

Bitachon

Every commandment has its expression. We express Passover by eating *matzah;* Shabbos by refraining from work; charity by giving money, etc. Practically speaking, how do we express our belief in this first Principle? How do we make it manifest in our lives?

Bitachon—reliance on G–d.[1]

The person with *bitachon* believes that nothing in the world happens by coincidence. People with *bitachon* do not panic. They do not ask, "What is going to be tomorrow?" because there is no tomorrow. G–d recreates each moment. And if a person believes that, why shouldn't he expect a miracle? Every second is a miracle. Nature is rejuvenated by G–d every moment. It is nothing more than a miracle repeated over and over again. True, an unrepeated miracle more easily catches our attention: G–d decides to interrupt the daily flow of natural miracles, and He has full control to do that whenever He wills.

---

[1] See Chapter 9, subchapter, "Bitachon and Chisayon."

The Creator

However, every second is also a miracle. We have simply gotten used to it. If so, then why not expect a miracle to take you out of adversity? Of course, we are not supposed to rely on miracles, but that does not mean one is not forthcoming.[1]

The person with *bitachon* does not look at nature as absolute. Nature is also a creation. It was created at the beginning of creation. However, at Mount Sinai nature was torn asunder. G–d said, "I am the G–d who took you out of Egypt, out of the house of bondage." I am not merely the G–d who created the world long ago. I am still intimately involved with the world—and My proof is that I am the G–d who performed all those miracles you saw in Egypt. True, I set up the original rules of nature at creation, but I am also capable of upsetting those rules whenever I so desire, and I desired to do so when I took you out of Egypt. Take this lesson to heart for all time that none of you need feel limited to the natural course of events. You who stand on Mount Sinai, and your descendants after you, are freed of that bondage—that state of mind which views nature as absolute. There are no absolute laws of "nature." Just because something happened yesterday does not mean it must happen today. I am the only absolute. Only Me. I alone ". . . made, make, and will make all things happen." Do not be deceived by nature and you may find the natural course of events flip-flopped for your sakes. Take this lesson to heart.

---

[1] And if one is not forthcoming, there too is a reason. See Chapter 9. And see *I Shall Not Want*, especially Chapter 3.

Beyond Survival

It is easy to talk about *bitachon,* but, admittedly, it is not easy to live it. Great people who live every moment as if it is a new creation make it seem easy. To them a miracle is not a surprise. The Talmud tells us about Rabbi Chanina ben Dosa, whose household had run out of oil for their lamps. He told his daughter to instead put vinegar in the lamps and, "Let He who makes oil burn, make the vinegar burn." And the vinegar burned. The simplicity of his faith was deceiving, though. It was really the result of years and years of hard work instilling in himself, over and over again, the belief that every moment is a new creation. For such a person miracles happen.

Great musicians seem to be naturals. Great artists seem to be naturals. Great athletes seem to be naturals. However, the truth is that people who became great at anything spent endless hours perfecting their craft. That is not always obvious to the outsider, but the biographies of such people reveal that whatever natural talent they were born with was worked on continually until it became natural.

A Jew's craft is first and foremost his *bitachon.* We only become great at it—and thereby worthy of the miracles such *bitachon* can produce—by endlessly telling and training ourselves in the belief that every moment is a new creation.

An atheist, by contrast, would somehow explain away the miracle of Chanina ben Dosa. It was a magic trick, a slight of hand. At best he would begrudgingly admit that

The Creator

it was a fluke, a one in a trillion coincidence. It was one of those unexplainable things that happens; nothing to make him change his views. A simple monotheist would go one step better and say that nature was broken. A holy man is able to persuade G–d to break nature.

However, we—believers in the Thirteen Principles—understand that there is no nature. Vinegar can burn just as naturally as oil. We are awed that oil burns. We do not let the fact that it burns every time we light it numb our sensitivities. We get excited over "everyday" happenings because we know that G–d is pumping into each moment renewed vitality. True, a miracle such as vinegar burning is even more exciting—we feel G–d's presence even more—but we do not let the "everyday" fool us into believing there is such a thing as nature.

One way to gauge our level of *bitachon* is to reflect on the way we think. For instance, when things suddenly go wrong most of us probably think, "How could such a thing happen? Why does G–d always do such things to me?" However, when things go smoothly we do not ask, "Why are things going so smoothly?" "Why did I make money?" "Why am I healthy?" We take it for granted that everything should go our way. We believe we deserve it. It is part of nature.

This kind of thinking contradicts true *bitachon*, which is founded upon this first of the Thirteen Principles. As the Rambam teaches in the opening statement to his magnum opus, the *Mishnah Torah*: "The foundation of all foundations, and the pillar of knowledge, is to know [and believe][1] that there exists a Primordial Existence who is the source of existence for all that exists." This present moment is not our doing, but G–d's. "He is the source of existence for all that exists." G–d is with us twenty-four hours a day. We just have to acknowledge that. If things go smoothly, can we take credit for it? And if they do not, do we have the right to give up hope? G–d made, makes, and will make all things happen.

This first Principle must be meditated upon daily. And it must be exercised regularly. We must continuously feel in contact with the real reality, with the fact that we are creations and that G–d is our Creator. He not only wants us to acknowledge Him during miraculous-style events, when we more easily and keenly feel His presence. He wants us to acknowledge Him now, to feel Him this moment, no matter how dark or mundane the moment is. He does not want us to treat Him as we treat a "spare tire"—something we use only when we are in trouble; something we forget about as long as things go smoothly. He wants a full-time relationship.

---

[1] See Chapter 1, Overview to *The Thirteen Principles*.

Chapter 3

Oneness And The Soul

CHAPTER 3

Oneness And The Soul

Principle 2: "I believe with perfect faith that the Creator is one. There is no oneness like His—at all. He alone is our G-d—He was, He is, He will be."

Principle 3: "I believe with perfect faith that the Creator is not a body. Physical concepts do not apply to Him. There is nothing comparable to Him at all."

Principle 4: "I believe with perfect faith that the Creator is the beginning and the end."

Physicists study two basic phenomena: space and time. Space is the material, physical world. All objects of the physical world occupy space; they exist within the basic dimensions of height, width, and breadth.

Time is the continuum of moments within which we live. Although less tangible than space, it too is something the mind can grasp. The common denominator between space and time is that they have a beginning, middle, and end.

How would we define something which has no beginning, middle, or end? The answer is that we cannot. There is no definition we can grasp which will explain it. The best we can do is explain what it is not. Timelessness is the absence of time. We cannot conceive of it in terms of a presence, but only an absence of that which we can grasp, namely time. We do have a term, eternity, but that is merely a label, not a definition we can conceive.

The only real way we can explain the statement that G–d is one is to say that it means He is not two. We cannot really grasp what it means to say He is one. We can only explain it by saying what He is not. He is not two. There are not two G-ds. The truth is, though, that there is obviously much more implied in the statement that G–d is one than the definition that He is not two. I just do not know if we can express it.

Even to say that G–d "was, is, and will always be" is an insufficient explanation. The concepts "was," "is," and "will" do not exist in a timeless framework. We simply cannot express it.

This thought, that G–d's oneness cannot be expressed within the concepts of space and time, is spelled out explicitly in the third and fourth Principles of Faith. The third Principle states:

Oneness And The Soul

"I believe with perfect faith that the Creator is not a body. There is nothing comparable to Him at all."

G–d is not physical. Space has no relationship to Him whatsoever. He cannot be understood by comparing Him to anything in the physical universe. Thus, this Principle teaches us about the infinite nature of G–d in relation to space.

The fourth Principle of Faith teaches about the infinite nature of G–d in relation to time:

"I believe with perfect faith that the Creator is the beginning and the end."

The sense here is that G–d is the beginning and end of all we can comprehend, but He Himself has no beginning or end. There was no time when G–d started to exist. Similarly, He has no end. Only physical properties have beginnings and ends. Creation may have a beginning and end, but the Creator does not.

Body And Soul

In the story of how the world came to be we find two creations. The first is symbolized by the word *beraishis*, "In the beginning." In the beginning, G–d created the entire physical universe, represented by the word "earth"[1]

---
[1] The entire spiritual realm was a creation as well. The word *shamayim*, "heaven," represents spirituality—all the elements of the spiritual world. In the beginning G–d created the entire spiritual

in the first verse of the Torah. But not only space; time, too, was created then.[1] "In the beginning" implies G–d created a beginning. Something happened that brought the universe into existence. Beforehand it did not exist.

Therefore, everything in existence outside of G–d—animals, angels, humans, matter, time, etc.—was all created through the utterance *beraishis*. It is the embryo of the universe. And that "embryo" has a specific date of birth, so to speak, the 25th day of the month of Elul, six days before the day we celebrate as Rosh HaShannah. Our Sages say (and it is stated explicitly by the Ramban) that *all* the raw material of the physical creation was created on that first day. Thus, after the word *beraishis* was said the ensuing six days accomplished nothing more than bringing to fruition the raw material which was created the first day.[2] Even the raw material of Adam's body existed on the first day.

---

realm as well.

[1] The Zohar says that the word *beraishis*, "In the beginning," can be read, *bara shis*, He created six, i.e. the six thousand years of physical creation. Similarly, the Vilna Gaon explains that the Five Books of the Torah contain all the events from the beginning of creation until the end of the 6,000th year, which in turn is condensed into the first two *parashios* (*Beraishis* and *Noach*, Genesis 1-11), which itself is condensed into the verses describing the six days of creation, which in turn is condensed into the very first word *beraishis*. Just as a fruit comes from a branch, which comes from a tree trunk which comes from a root which comes from a seed, so, too, the first word is the seed of all creation. And just as, theoretically, a scientist could see in the seed the eventual tree and its fruit in their entirety, so, too, if we would have a spiritual microscope and the insight, we would be able to determine all history in its entirety from the first word, *beraishis*.

[2] Nothing described as coming into existence during the first six days of creation (after the first word *beraishis* was spoken) can be

Oneness And The Soul

After that first creation, on the 25th of Elul, came a second one. This second creation is what occurred six days later, Rosh HaShannah. The Torah says, "And G–d created man in His image; in the image of G–d He created him..."[1] The man created in the image of G–d is not the man created on the first day with that first utterance, *beraishis*. Man in the image of G–d is the creation elaborated upon by the verse, "And He blew into him an everlasting soul."[2] Through that act of blowing, G–d actually instilled a part of Himself into the physical man.[3] That "creation" did not need an embryonic unfolding of events. It was performed in one instant.[4]

---

called a creation. Rather they are only formations. The word creation means that something which never existed first gets brought into existence. A carpenter does not *create* a table. He merely *makes* a table. He uses wood and material already in existence, and then forms them into a table. So too everything after the first words *beraishis bara*. And that is why the word "create" (*bara*) is only used once in the description of creation. Everything else was "made" (*asa*) from the raw material brought into existence by *beraishis*. [The exception to this concerns the creation of the *taninim*, the "serpents." The commentators deal with this exception. It does not serve our purpose here to delve into why the word *bara* is used in that instance instead of *asa*.]

[1] Gen. 1:27
[2] Ibid. 2:7.
[3] "One who breathes into another person gives into him something of his own essence." (Ramban, ibid.)
[4] The difference between an unfolding of events versus an instantaneous occurrence (evolution versus revolution) is the difference between body and soul, as well as the difference between speech and simply "blowing," as I am about to explain.

The Sages tell us that there were ten levels of constriction, ten utterances, through which the world was created. An utterance is like an electricity transformer. An electrical generator produces millions of kilowatts of electricity. A transformer reduces the voltage so that you can plug your appliance into a socket. Of course, one transformer

Beyond Survival

Thus, we are in reality two creations in one: a body and a soul. The body came to be with the utterance, *beraishis*. The soul came to reside inside us with the act of blowing (represented by the words, "... and He blew...."). The body is bound by space and time. The soul is unbounded.

---

is not enough to give your vacuum cleaner the proper amount of electricity. A second transformer, a third transformer, and so on are needed until the energy flowing through the line is safe for household use.

The original statement *beraishis* was infused with such high degrees of "G-dliness" that it needed to be transformed into levels usable for His creations. There were ten such "transformers," which are represented by the words, "And G-d said..." Each one further reduced and transformed the original utterance. The tenth utterance was the one containing the least potent voltage of "G-dliness." That tenth saying was the creation of man. Man possesses the greatest reduction of "G-dliness"—he is composed of the darkest matter—in the sense that he has the potential to deny G-d. (By contrast, "And G-d said, Let there be light..." was the second utterance [the Talmud considers the first word *beraishis* as an utterance]. Thus light is the greatest symbol of G-d. Torah is called light. It is light that lets one "see the light." Light is the most ethereal of physical substances, the closest thing to G-d the natural world possesses.)

Nevertheless, despite being a product of the tenth, most physical utterance, G-d gave man the potential to become the highest element of creation, in fact to transcend creation: the divine image, the everlasting soul that was "blown" into man. Note that the verse does not say, "And G-d said, I will blow the everlasting soul into man." It is simply, "And G-d blew..." He "blew" into man a part of Himself.

Who am I? How was I made? My physical part was made with the tenth utterance. My spiritual part was not made with any utterance. It was simply "blown" into me. An utterance is something intended for a listener. Speech is a reduction of thought, a necessary reduction for the sake of communication, but a reduction nonetheless. The act of blowing represented an unrestricted transference of G-d's being into a part of creation, man.

Oneness And The Soul

The body is a creation of G–d. The soul is a portion of G–d.

Is it possible to comprehend the statement that G–d deposited an actual part of Himself into us? I do not believe so. Yet, that is the import of what the Torah says.

Still, we can try to explain it. Imagine our heads were computers and I had a disk containing a beautiful, complex program I wanted to show you. I could show you the program by bringing it up on the monitor screen and by letting you read it piecemeal, page by page. Or I could just put the disk into the slot in your head. In such a transference, the receiver receives my entire thought.

G–d gave us two ways to comprehend His existence: The first way through *beraishis*, the physical creation in which we can discern piecemeal exactly how G–d came to be in the unfolding of the world. The second way is instantaneous, through connecting with the part of G–d which He simply put into us in one shot.

My body is a product of *beraishis*. My soul, on the other hand, is a unified whole. It cannot be broken into parts. I cannot even explain it. Just because the "disk" was slid into my head does not mean I can grasp it like my rational mind grasps the divinity of creation. Yet because it is there I can intuit its presence to a degree even my rational mind cannot grasp.

My physical self is limited. But my soul is unlimited; it is a disk with an infinite amount of information. True, in this world it is impossible to fully develop the information. We are too limited. But the seed of eternity already resides within us. And we have been given the mechanism of cultivating that seed: the Torah. Our purpose here, now, is one of process; we are trying to remove the limits imposed by creation; we are peeling back the layers within which hide the essential core.

According to the Sages, a fetus is taught the entire Torah in the womb by an angel. Then, at birth, the angel touches the child on the lip, which causes him to forget all he had learned.[1] The obvious question is: If the fetus forgets it all, what was the purpose of teaching him in the first place? The answer is that some impression remains forever; the Torah is still there, but it is lost to consciousness. And from that impression the maturing adult can reconstruct what he had learned. Reconstructing an impression is a much more promising endeavor than learning it for the first time. We don't forget the essence of the eternal soul. It is always there. We just have to bring it from our subconscious into our consciousness through the process of learning Torah, through a process which must take place within time.

There are two creations, then. One is *beraishis*, a creation within time and space. The other—the creation created on Rosh HaShannah—is true eternity; it is above time and space.

---

[1] *Niddah* 30b.

Oneness And The Soul

Who Am I?

This leads to the number one problem facing each of us. We each have an identity crisis. We don't know who we are. Are we physical or spiritual? We feel yearnings for both simultaneously. And it is an unavoidable conflict. We are a product of two creations: the physical creation (*beraishis*) and the spiritual infusion ("... and He blew...."); the body and the soul.

Animals do not have identity crises. Physical matter is not conflicted over its true nature. We are different. By our very natures we are mixed up—unless we clearly establish one over the other. Who am I? When I identify myself with my soul, I share in the attributes of G–d's image. What is true for G–d has truth for the soul. When we say that G–d beyond time and not physical, we are saying that those attributes are in us. We are not physical. We are not divisible. We are one. We are whole. We are unique. The more we know G–d, then, the more we know ourselves; the more we know our true selves—the part of G–d within us.

Our great life mission is to voluntarily identify ourselves with our soul.[1] That, in fact, underlies the unique service we perform on Rosh HaShannah: the "blowing" of shofar. By blowing the shofar we are demonstrating our true identity. We are declaring that we are not first and foremost products of *beraishis*. We are products of G–d's "blowing" into us an everlasting soul. Just as He blew a soul into us (on the original Rosh HaShannah),

---

[1] See Chapter 8, subsection, "Citizenship."

Beyond Survival

we blow the shofar to show that we define ourselves as souls.

There are two ways we can look at ourselves, then. The first is as a physical person who will live hopefully to eighty or longer. However, can such a person really appreciate each moment of life? After all, in the context of a full lifetime is the present moment an accomplishment? Before our days are over we fail so often and in so many ways. And even when we succeed, can we honestly say that we have reached the full potential an eighty or ninety year lifetime is meant to produce?

On the other hand, when we view ourselves as everlasting souls, then we are fully accomplished this moment. G–d does not exist within time. Every moment is an eternity unto itself. Each breath we take is infinitely precious and valuable. Consequently, a person should never despair. Every split second of life, no matter how successful or unsuccessful, is a part of eternity itself. Only in a physical sense can we fail. But in a "soul" sense we can never fail because the soul is not dependent upon action. It is part of eternity; its very being is a success.

The more despair, the greater the proof that we have not settled our identity crisis. We may tell ourselves we are souls, but do we really believe it if we let life's continually changing fortunes destabilize, depress, or overwhelm us? Failure, suffering—and ultimately death—are eventualities each of us must confront. But those stark realities only exist in terms of *beraishis*, in terms of the

Oneness And The Soul

physical creation. Our uniqueness is the deposit of G–d in us. If we live up to that, we need never despair.

Isn't that a beautiful message? Why is it, then, that we forget it? Why do we let life's predicaments get to us?

Let me explain the reason with an analogy. Suppose G–d proposed to you two ways of resolving all your financial dilemmas. The mortgage, the car loan, the tuition, your children's wedding expenses, etc.—will all be solved. But, you have a choice of which way to solve your financial problems. The first is that G–d will deposit in a Swiss bank account in your name $100 million. And you have full access to it whenever you want. It is yours. The second way is that He will give you one penny. However, that penny will double itself continually. One, two, four, eight, sixteen, thirty-two, etc.—endlessly. Now, which way would you pick? The $100 million or the penny? The answer is obvious: we would all pick the penny. It looks smaller, but it is really worth more.

However, let us add a twist. Suppose your house is under foreclosure, they are coming to repossess your car, you owe money to many impatient people, etc. Which would you choose now? The $100 million or the penny? The $100 million, most people would admit. Why? Because the penny needs time to develop into a substantial sum and you need the money NOW! You won't see the profits of the penny for a while. So, you say to yourself, "I'll be satisfied with the large sum of money up front."

Of course, you just gave up eternal wealth for a mere $100 million.

Beyond Survival

Let me break the news to you. We forego the constantly multiplying penny regularly in our lives, but for much less than 100 million dollars, or even a thousand dollars. In fact, that was Adam's sin (the sin he perpetrated on Rosh HaShannah). G–d put him in the Garden of Eden with two trees at its center: the Tree of Life and the Tree of Knowledge. The former tree bestowed eternal life. The latter tree bestowed knowledge—$100 million worth of knowledge, but a limited knowledge nonetheless. The value of the Tree of Life was beyond rationality. It was beyond knowledge. It was eternal. The knowledge represented by the Tree of Knowledge was a temptation of the moment. It was incredibly desirable, but ultimately limited.

Adam of course chose to eat from the latter and as a result he brought upon himself and his descendants death, the limitation of life. Adam chose the $100 million cash over the ever-multiplying penny.[1] He chose the physical creation, *beraishis*, over the instantaneous one, "... and He blew."

The first responsibility each of us has is to identify who we are. We are each an everlasting soul. And we must never forget this. One way to remember this fact is to meditate on it regularly... everyday. And we have many teachings designed for just such meditation. For instance, every morning we say *Elokai neshama*:

---

[1] The Arizal writes that had Adam waited until night he would have received the Tree of Knowledge's knowledge in any event.

Oneness And The Soul

"My G–d, the soul that You put in me is pure. You created it, You formed it, You blew it into me, and You preserve it within me...."

Meditate on that for a few minutes each morning and your day will be different. And I am not talking about kabbalistic meditation. I am talking about simply thinking about the words: "My G–d, the soul that you put in me is pure." G–d, You put it into me not through words, but in one action. It is not something I need to develop. It already exists within me whole. It is the full "disk."

"You created it [the soul], You formed it, and You blew it into me ..." One who breathes into another person gives into him something of his own essence. You blew a part of Yourself into me. You are in me.

"And you preserve it within me." That means that at this very moment, as you read these words, G–d is watching over the soul that is within you. It is not natural for a soul to exist in a body. Spiritual things gravitate toward spiritual things, and physical things toward physical things. The fact that your soul stays within you requires a special act of "guarding over" on G–d's part. If He thought it was not important He would simply stop preserving it and let it fly out of your body. But He does not withdraw His guard, because it is very important to Him that your soul be in you now. And He does that for the trillions of split seconds which comprise your life. Every trillionth of a second is an entire creation, an entire eternity. It is a gift. It is G–d Himself in us.

Beyond Survival

Meditate on this Principle of Faith daily. It is fundamental, not only for belief but for a healthy state of mind, for your basic well-being. You can never feel devastated when you make this belief a real part of you.

Summary

We covered a lot in this chapter, not the least of which is the commandment to unify G–d's name (*yichud Hashem*). Unifying G–d's name is the purpose of the "Shma Yisroel," which we are commanded to say twice daily (once in the morning and once in the evening). Next time you say it, say it with the understanding laid out in this chapter:

Shma Yisroel — "Listen Israel," which means understand, be aware, pay attention, meditate and reflect deeply;

Hashem Elokeinu — "G–d" in the aspect of *Havaya*—not merely *Elokim* and *Sha–dai*, but *Havaya*, the G–d who recreates every instant, who energizes our entire existence—"is our G–d;"

Hashem Echad — "G–d is one." He is not divisible into parts. He is whole. The entire creation—all time, and every space—cannot compare to a split second of G–d's oneness, a oneness which is manifest in my life by virtue of His blowing the eternal soul into me and preserving it there.

Chapter 4

Prayer

CHAPTER 4

Prayer

Principle 5: "I believe with perfect faith that to the Creator—to Him alone—is it appropriate to pray. It is not appropriate to pray to another."

If we truly believed that G–d listened to our every word of prayer we would pray day and night. In fact, we might even seek to attain that perpetual state of prayer embodied by David who said, *v'ani tefillah*, "I am prayer." How many of us, though, do not possess anything approaching that level of appreciation for prayer? Why is it that so often our prayers seem burdensome and insincere? Why is it that so many people do not pray at all—and I am not referring only to non-believers, but those who believe in G–d; why is it that there are so many people who go days, weeks, and months without uttering a sincere word of prayer?

The answer boils down to one of two reasons: a lack of self-confidence or an excess of self-confidence. The first type of people believe that G–d does not want to be bothered with their petty problems. They rationalize, "Who am I that G–d should listen to me?" The second

Beyond Survival

type believe that prayer serves no purpose if G–d knows what they want anyway. They rationalize, "Since G–d knows everything, what use is there in praying?"

Both reasons are wrong because, first and foremost, we pray because G–d commanded us to pray. It makes no difference how insignificant we think we are. And it makes no difference that G–d knows our needs. We have an obligation to pray. That obligation extends so far that even if we know how the future will turn out we are not relieved of the responsibility to turn to G–d in prayer.[1]

The Brisker Rav was known to murmur words under his breath whenever people in need came to him and told him their problems. When asked why he did that, he responded, "Whenever a person tells me his pain it hurts me too. The minute I feel that pain the requirement of the Torah to pray falls upon me. So, immediately I say under my breath, Please, Almighty, help this person." He saw it as *his* requirement to pray whenever he felt another's pain. How much more so, then, must we pray for ourselves whenever we feel pain. Therefore, the first point to keep in mind is that prayer is an obligation.

---

[1] On the verse, "And Mordechai knew all that was done" (Esther 4:1) the Sfas Emes (*Purim*, 5634) explains that Mordechai knew in advance that Haman's decree to exterminate the Jews would not be carried out. Even so, he still prayed (and gathered together all the Jews to pray for their lives) as if he had not known the future. Additionally, the Sfas Emes adds, that perhaps is what defines a true *tzaddik* (righteous person). The *tzaddik* is someone to whom G–d will show the future because He knows that that foreknowledge will not hinder him from praying as if he knew nothing.

Prayer

Personal rationales and weaknesses have no bearing on that obligation.

Unfortunately, when difficulty strikes the first address we look up is usually not G–d's—at least not right away. We go over to a friend, look up the doctor's telephone number, seek out an influential person, etc. G–d is our last resource, not the first. Yet, "He alone" is the appropriate source to whom we must first seek help. His is the only address. The first thing we must do, then, is pray to G–d and cast our burdens upon Him. After that we can turn to others, because then they become nothing but agents for G–d's answer to our prayers. Perhaps it is G–d's will that we will be helped through that other person. But they are not the ones upon whom we rely. "He alone" is the source of help.

"It is not appropriate to pray to another." We are accustomed to going to holy sites to pray: the Wall, the Tomb of Rachel, the graves of holy people, etc. It is a good practice, but it is not the deceased holy people to whom we should address our prayers. Rather we are praying to G–d. However, we say, "In the merit of such and such person, please, G–d, listen to me." The holy person buried there serves as a better connection, but he is *not* the party to whom we speak.

And the same holds true in terms of going to living holy people for blessings. The obligation is on us to pray. The holy person can only help our prayers to reach their mark. Compare it to a person who is physically hungry. He does not go to another person and say, "Please eat for me." He eats the food himself. The other person can perhaps help him obtain food, but not eat it for him. Genuine *tzaddikim*, holy people, pray that our prayers be acceptable. They do not do the praying for us.

The story is told about one of the Chassidic Rebbes who would periodically demand money from various people who sought him out to pray in their behalf. In fact, whenever he demanded money it was almost a guaranteed sign that the person's request would be fulfilled. As the story goes, one time a penniless widow approached this Rebbe because she needed money to marry off her children. "Only your blessing can help me," she cried bitterly.

"I will pray for you," he replied, "if you first give me 5,000 kroner," which was an exorbitant sum.

"Rebbe," she said stunned, "I am a poor widow. Where am I going to come up with 5,000 kroner?"

"I am sorry. Without the 5,000 kroner I cannot help you."

She almost became hysterical. "If I were to sell my entire house and liquidate everything in it," she said, "I still couldn't put together 5,000 kroner."

"I am sorry," he replied. "I cannot help you without the 5,000 kroner."

Seeing he would not budge, she decided that she would try bargaining with him. "Maybe if I sell everything I can put together 1,000 kroner. I will give you the entire sum, but please answer my prayer for 1,000 kroner."

Prayer

"I am sorry," he said stone-faced. "5,000 kroner or nothing."

At that point she became furious. "This is the way a Rebbe behaves?! This is the way you treat a poor widow?!" After her tirade, she calmed down a little and said, "What can the Rebbe do, anyway? All he can do is say some prayers for me. You know what, I am going to keep my money and instead pray for myself!"

"Ah!" the Rebbe said, "that is what I was waiting to hear. Now I give you a blessing that you be helped."

The moral is that we have to pray only to G–d. From the beginning, the Rebbe realized that the woman did not understand that and so he cleverly led her to come to that conclusion on her own. We have to realize the same thing. "It is not appropriate to pray to another."

And this is a particularly great test nowadays. More than ever, the world appears to run on its own. A person gets a headache. Does he pray to G–d? No, the first instinct is to go to the medicine cabinet and take some aspirin. Nevertheless, any time we have a need, even as minor as a headache, we are required to turn to G–d. And the underlying reason is because dependence on G–d creates our relationship with Him. In fact, that is why He made us with so many needs. Animals are created with most of their needs and instincts intact. Nature takes good care of them. Humans are the most complex creatures and we have the most complex demands. G–d created us that way so we would have the greatest cause to turn to Him, to grab hold of His hand, so to speak.

Beyond Survival

And it is probably because we do have so many needs that we feel awkward bothering Him with them. They seem so petty at times. However, G-d wants us to be a "nudge." He wants us to get used to turning toward Him for everything from relief of our headaches to fulfillment of our deepest dreams. It is possible—and indeed ideal—to turn to G-d every second. In so doing, we live with Him twenty-four hours a day. That is the goal.

Therefore, it is wrong to not pray to G-d because we think our requests are too small. We should not belittle ourselves. We have to acknowledge that we are worthy to come before G-d to speak to Him. And we must train ourselves to turn to Him for everything. We have to get used to speaking to Him as we speak to our parents. That is how we develop a living faith in His presence.

The second reason why some people, consciously or subconsciously, do not turn to G-d is based on an entirely different motive: they have so much faith—or, so they think—that they take G-d for granted. Why pray, they rationalize, when G-d knows what I need anyway? Whatever He wants to give me He will give me. And whatever He does not want to give me I will not get no matter how much I pray. What's the use?

The fault with that attitude is that G-d created us with certain feelings and desires. We were created to be afraid of impending danger. If a SCUD missile is going to land in your neighborhood in the next thirty seconds something would be wrong with you if you were not afraid. Faith cannot be used as an excuse for deep-seated

Prayer

insensitivity toward life—others lives or your own. You were created with feelings to remind you to talk to and beseech G–d when the situation calls for it.

G–d created each of us deficient in one way or another, as well as with a sensitivity to our deficiencies, because He wants us to turn to Him to get them filled. Therefore, it is very important to have wants. We are not supposed to deny them. Wants obligate us to turn to G–d in prayer. Faith which totally benumbs a person's instinctual feelings is really just another name for recklessness. Such "faith" probably extends from laziness—an inherent apathy which naturally manifests itself in carelessness and negligence. In order to justify that apathy such a person claims to possess faith in G–d. "I owe money—so what? Who cares? Why should I lose sleep over it? Why should I pray any extra. G–d knows what I need." That type of faith is reckless because it comes at the expense of others, be it a spouse, family member, friend, business associate, etc. The proper attitude requires the most delicate of balances. It is perhaps the most difficult challenge facing us. We must have faith, yet at the same time we must feel and behave normally. We must put forth normal effort to fulfill our needs.

In conclusion, then, both too little confidence in who we are and too much confidence fail us. We are never relieved of the obligation to pray—neither because we think our needs are too petty nor because we think G–d will take care of our needs anyway. We have to walk that thin line, that narrow bridge, as long as we live.

The Global Effect

The Mishnah[1] states: "On three pillars the world stands: On Torah, on *Avodah* (Divine "service"), and *Gemilus Chasadim* (loving-kindness)." We can relatively easily understand how the world cannot stand or exist without Torah. The world has a destiny. Torah, knowledge of the world from the Creator's vantage point, instructs us in detail how to perform our part in bringing about that destiny. Without Torah, the goal of creation could not be attained. If so, the world would literally cease to exist.

Likewise, we can understand the absolute need for *Gemilus Chasadim*. G-d does not need anything. He only created (and maintains) the world from the purest motivation to give,[2] as the Torah teaches, "The kindness of G-d [supports the world] all day."[3] If people do not allow Him to give, then the entire purpose of creation is frustrated and the world thereby loses its reason for existence.[4] *Gemilus Chasadim*, therefore, is literally a pillar of

---

[1] Avos 1:2.
[2] Addressing the question: Why did G-d create the world? the Arizal explained that since G-d is by definition good, and *the nature of good is to want to give good to another*, He created an "other" in order bestow good upon. Creation is that other.
[3] Psalms 52:3.
[4] Since G-d created the world in order to give (see footnote 2), then the greatest function of the world is to act as a recipient of the good the Creator wants to bestow. That is the supreme human purpose. We are here to allow G-d to give to us; to earn reward by performing His will (see *To Become One*, Chapter 2). In that sense, then, a creation can bestow *Gemilus Chasadim* on his Creator. We can give to G-d by allowing Him to give to us.

Such a reciprocating cycle of give-and-take justifies our reason for

Prayer

the world, because the world exists specifically to allow G–d to do kindness.

The difficult point to understand, however, concerns *Avodah*. *Avodah* refers to prayer, "the service of the heart," as the Sages teach. Is prayer really a pillar of the world? Does it play as vital a metaphysical role as Torah and *Gemilus Chasadim*?

---

existence. However, should the cycle be discontinued—were one to make it impossible for G–d to bestow good on him—that person would be frustrating the entire purpose of creation, and thereby forfeit his reason for existence. That explains the underlying dynamic behind the destruction of Sodom. The essence of Sodom's evil is captured in a Talmudic teaching: "One who says, 'What is mine is mine, and what is yours is yours,' is an average person [neither righteous nor wicked]; others contend that this attitude resembles the manner of Sodom." Defining the attitude of "what's mine is mine" as "the manner of Sodom" is surprising. "What's mine is mine" may not be an overly righteous attitude, but can it be associated with Sodom, the society notorious for evil? After all, that attitude demands nothing of anyone else and even says, "What's yours is yours." However, the Maharal explains that such an individual does not say, "What's yours is yours" out of generosity. Rather, he says it because his entire mindset is self-centered; he only lets the other person retain what he has in order to retain his right to say, "What's mine is mine." On the outside, therefore, he appears to be a decent person, yet on the inside his entire orientation is toward selfishness.

That summarizes the people of Sodom. The *Midrash* (*Pirkei D'rebbi Eliezer*) shows how even their welfare system was nothing but a front for selfishness. And there were many such examples (see our discussion in Part II of *Days Are Coming*). In effect, then, Sodom succeeded in completely outlawing *Gemilus Chasadim*, a situation which made it impossible for G–d to bestow good on them. Without that reciprocating cycle of give-and-take between Creator and creation, one of the "pillars" necessary for their continued existence no longer existed. The natural result was the collapse of their world. In the deepest sense, then, the destruction of Sodom was not so much a punishment as a cause and effect.

Beyond Survival

The key to a answering that question is found in the following verse: "... and no greenery of the field had yet grown, for G-d had not caused it to rain upon the earth, and man did not exist yet to toil (*la'avod*) the fields."[1] The word used for "toil" is *la'avod* (i.e. *Avodah*). Thus, Rashi comments that the reason G-d did not cause it to rain at first was because He wanted Adam to "toil" (i.e. pray) for it. When Adam prayed, Rashi explains, the rain promptly fell and caused the greenery to begin growing. The great lesson the Torah is teaching, therefore, is that prayer is the mechanism of rain, and, in a larger sense, for all blessing which comes to the world.

Prayer is the mechanism by which the blessings of heaven come down to the earth. G-d created heaven and earth in such a way that they are not necessarily connected. Everything we need in our physical lives has been long ago prepared and "prepackaged," ready to be delivered to our doorstep. However, it is locked up in the heavens. Prayer opens the storehouses of blessing otherwise closed to our access.[2]

---

[1] Gen. 2:5.
[2] Of course, that does not mean that the real benefit of prayer is getting what one asked for. Rather the process of turning to G-d for whatever we need opens up channels through which we can receive *what G-d wants to give us*. To illustrate: Saul originally approached the prophet Samuel with a request to help him locate his father's lost sheep. The prophet told him to not worry about the sheep. Rather, the Jewish people needed a King and G-d had chosen Saul.
So, too, with us. Sometimes we ask G-d for something and it does not seem to have been answered. However, "no prayer returns empty." Every heart-felt request of G-d makes a connection. And even if our request is not answered directly it makes a connection

Prayer

Another way of looking at it is that prayer is like a light switch. Flipping the switch completes a circuit which makes a connection between a bulb and the generator at the local electric plant. So, too, prayer connects us to the heavenly storehouses of blessing. It is the light switch which is capable of closing the circuit between heaven and earth.

Beyond the benefits to the individual, though, prayer is designed to bestow universal benefits. Every human being has a specific assignment to bring down blessing into this world. The world will not reach its completion until its individuals "flip on" their respective "light switches."[1] Thus, over and above our personal needs, prayer is essential for the ultimate development of the entire world. And that explains why prayer, *Avodah*, literally "service" (of G-d), is a pillar of the world. Prayer which serves a global need directly impacts on creation, not just on the individual. It is an act which literally serves G-d in that it directly feeds into the grand design of His creation.

This is a vitally important point to understand deeply, so let me explain it more fully. The distinction between prayer which serves an individual need versus prayer which produces a global impact can be compared to the distinction between Leah and Rachel.[2] Leah represents

---

which allows us to receive true blessing. In fact, sometimes a request to find the whereabouts of "lost sheep" is responded to with the news that G-d has "appointed us King."

[1] See Chapter 7, *The Coming of the Messiah*.

[2] It is not coincidence that two women serve as a paradigm for prayer. Just as Torah study is the primary responsibility of the man, prayer (in its informal, more vital sense) is the primary responsibility

prayer for local, individual needs. As the Sages tell us, her eyes were not as beautiful as Rachel's because she continually cried out in prayer that G–d avert the decree that she marry Esau. And G–d did. She prayed to G–d to give her children. And He did. Her prayers produced immediate results. Prayers which are answered immediately, or relatively quickly, usually extend from a local need, one that is vital to an individual's personal life circumstances.

Rachel, on the other hand, represents the global person. She did not have her prayers answered immediately, and thus went childless for many years. Rachel's global nature was summarized by the prophet who wrote, "Rachel is crying over her children,"[1] for all Jewish children, which was said in reference to the Jewish exiles who were led past Rachel's burial spot on their way to slavery in Babylon. Rachel's prayers were plugged into global needs. To best illustrate this point, consider the following story I heard first hand.

In the early 1940s, Rav Hillel Slesinger was in Palestine by Rachel's burial spot. A group of secular

---

of the woman. (Of course, a man must pray and a woman must study to know her Torah obligations, but the point here is merely one of primary emphasis.) Thus, for instance, the Talmud deduces the laws of prayer from Hannah, the mother of the prophet Samuel. A woman's heart can more easily be deeply touched than a man's, and thus she is the paradigm of prayer, the service of the heart. Consequently, regarding Torah and prayer—two of the three pillars which "hold up the world"—a man and a woman share equally. They are equal partners in running the overall system of creation.

[1] Jeremiah 31:14.

Prayer

kibbutzniks approached. One of the women, apparently a recent refugee from Hitler's Germany, began praying. She prayed loud enough in her native German for Rav Hillel to overhear. This completely assimilated woman, who did not even know Hebrew, prayed: "Mother Rachel, you know the pain of not having children... and you are the one who can feel my pain from all these years of being childless. Only you can help me. Pray for me." The prayer was so genuine, Rav Hillel thought, that he was convinced it would eventually be answered. A year later, he called up the kibbutz to find out if anything had happened to the woman. Indeed, they informed him, she had given birth. Rachel's supplications traveled 3,000 years to a non-religious woman! That is a global prayer.

We have to realize that there is a Rachel in all of us. And that is why we should never be frustrated if there is a deep, painful need we live with daily which does not seem to be getting met. Certain needs of ours may in reality be portents of global needs. Like Rachel, one may be childless for many years and wonder why her prayers are not answered when at the same time a friend has child after child. The answer is that a Rachel's individual need is in reality a global need. The individual, local need (for example, childlessness) was merely given to the individual in order to produce prayers which would have a global impact. Consequently, G–d does not fulfill such prayers immediately. He is listening every bit as much, and even more so, to those prayers. However, He refrains from answering them in an immediately satisfactory way because He wants those prayers to continue in their full intensity.[1]

In summary, then, we all have needs which compel us to turn to G–d to have them met. However, there are two types of needs. Certain needs are related to personal, local scenarios. Prayers for those needs tend to be answered relatively quickly. At the same time, we may have

---

[1] Even if an individual need is never seemingly met, we have a principle that prayers never go unanswered. How? Consider the following example as one possible answer. Imagine a couple who had given birth to fifteen children and 300 grandchildren. They go to heaven and are informed that they really only brought into the world three children and thirty grandchildren.

"What about the other twelve children and 270 grandchildren?" they ask.

"You never prayed for them. In fact, you prayed that you should not have them. Of course, you could not go against My wishes. I had to 'smuggle' those souls into this world despite your wishes. I can give you credit for baby-sitting, for the price of diapers, etc. However, I cannot give you credit for the children themselves because you never prayed for them. You never wanted them."

Next, a childless couple comes before G–d in the World to Come. All their life, they prayed day and night for children, but never had them. Nevertheless, they are informed, "We consider it as if you had 3,000 children and 10,000 grandchildren."

"How could that be? We did not even have one child!"

"True. However, there were twelve unwanted, unprayed-for children from the previous couple who were here. In addition to those twelve children, there were five from another couple, three from yet another, seven from yet another, etc. All of those children really came into the world as a result of your efforts and prayers. Therefore, in essence, they are yours."

Prayers are always answered, but sometimes only somewhere else in ways we do not know. In the next world, however, we will be shown where each and every prayer was answered. Thus, regardless of how hopeless the situation looks, one should never lose hope and stop praying. Every prayer returns paid-in-full, one way or another, sooner or later.

Prayer

a part of us attached global needs. In that case, the personal need is merely a front for a much more encompassing need, and therefore may not be answered so quickly.

Given that understanding, now we can truly perceive why prayer is one of the Thirteen Principles. Prayer is not merely a tool for the individual. Prayer is a means of affecting truly global changes, of nothing less than completing the work of creation. In fact, the wording in this Principle, "To Him alone it is appropriate to pray," takes on a new shade of meaning. Not only does it mean that G-d is the only One to whom we must direct our prayers, as we explained before. But it can also be understood, "*For* Him alone it is appropriate to pray." In other words, our prayers should ideally be motivated for G-d's sake, *tefillah lishmah*. G-d's sake—His "need," so to speak—is that His creation be brought to completion. For that, He needs not only our Torah and *Gemilus Chasadim*, but our *Avodah* (i.e. prayer), as well.

Chapter 5

The Message

CHAPTER 5

The Message

Principle 6: "I believe with perfect faith that all the words of the prophets are true."

Principle 7: "I believe with perfect faith that the prophecy of Moshe (Moses) our teacher was absolutely true. He was the father of all prophets, those who came before him and those who came after him."

Principle 8: "I believe with perfect faith that the Torah which we have today in our hands is the actual Torah given to Moshe our teacher."

Principle 9: "I believe with perfect faith that the Torah will not be changed and there will never be any other Torah given by the Creator."

The sixth, seventh, eighth and ninth Principles of Faith form one basic unit. The theme flows naturally from the previous Principles, which first told us that there is a Creator and that we can communicate with that Creator. This next group—the subject of this chapter—tells us in effect that the Creator has used this "communication link-up" to give us a message which amounts to nothing less than the entire purpose of creation, namely Torah. Let us analyze these Principles one at a time.

The simple understanding of the sixth Principle is that we have to believe that "all the words of the prophets are true," meaning the words of all the prophets in the twenty-four books of *Tanach*.[1] However, there is a broader implication here: G–d speaks to human beings.[2] Moreover, not only did He speak to human beings long ago, but He did not stop speaking to human beings with the death of the last prophet, Malachi. He continues to transmit His Torah even today.

Admittedly, true prophecy ceased with the last prophets after our return from exile in Babylon and Persia, and anyone who claims to possess instructions from G–d with the same authority as the prophets of old is a fraud. Nevertheless, lower levels of transmission (such as *ruach hakodesh*, *bas kol*, etc.) continue to operate.[3] Therefore, just as we know that the authentic interpretation of the Torah (i.e. the oral Torah) did not cease with the death of Moshe—but was passed on to the Elders and then to

---
[1] I.e. Scripture: *T*orah, *N*eviim (the Prophets), *K*esuvim (the Writings).
[2] "It is a principle of our faith that G–d grants prophecy to human beings." (Rambam, *Yesoday HaTorah* 7:1)
[3] *Moreh Nevuchim*.

The Message

the Prophets, et al.[1]—there is an authentic voice of the Torah today, namely our living sages.

Simple reflection upon the style of the written Torah leads to that understanding. The written Torah (the Five Books) is not very explicit. It was clearly designed to be a general guide, a text to be interpreted in order to extract the true depth of its message. And it was clearly intended to be universal and timeless, something that would speak to all generations, under all circumstances, all the time. Obviously, then, the Author had in mind to speak to worthy living human beings, who would interpret it, throughout *all* the generations. Thus, the idea of *daas Torah*, an authentic Torah position as interpreted by living authorities, is part and parcel of a written Torah.

Other religions and indeed many non-observant Jews claim to believe the written Torah, but not the Torah espoused by the rabbis as laid forth in the oral Torah, the Talmud. There is a primal human motivation underlying such claims: the need to be one's own authority. Once one has the right to disbelieve a Torah authority one becomes one's own authority. There is really no responsibility except to one's self. And thus the need to undermine the authority of the oral Torah is a basic part of human psychology.

In all fairness the mistake is not difficult to make because the written Torah is indeed very general. It is really only the tip of the iceberg of a much fuller body of knowledge and conduct given by G–d to the Jewish

---

[1] Avos 1:1.

Beyond Survival

People on Mount Sinai. Perceptive people realize, however, that if G-d gave the tip of an iceberg He must have also given a much larger mass of ice beneath the surface.[1] That mass is the oral Torah as transmitted from generation to generation, father to son, teacher to disciple. One who is not committed to listen to his teachers—teachers who listened to their teachers, and so on—not only has no oral Torah, but has no Torah. Period. A Torah designed to fit one's lifestyle according to one's own perceptions is not Torah.

Such people contend, though, that the Torah of the oral law is not Torah either, substantiating their words with the claim even the rabbis disagreed with each other on various points. "They can't all be right," such people say. "Therefore, doesn't that disprove your claim to possessing the authentic Torah?"

The answer is that the rabbis agree in essence: the Torah is from Sinai; it is Divine; it consists of 613 commandments; every Jew is obligated to keep the entire Torah; the Talmud is the repository of the oral law which was given on Sinai and transmitted from generation to generation; the Shulchan Aruch is the codification of the oral law; etc. They differ only in respect to certain particulars.

---

[1] The analogy of the iceberg should not be misconstrued to imply that the oral Torah does not exist in the written Torah. Everything is in the written Torah, but the oral Torah is the only authoritative source from whence the details of the written Torah are properly extracted and applied.

The Message

But even in respect to the difference of opinion regarding certain particulars the authenticity of the claim is not undermined. Compare it to a single human body, which is made up of many different organs and systems. Some parts even oppose each other. Certain glands produce sugar while others produce insulin which counteracts the effects of sugar. Health is a function of the proper balance between the disparate parts, not the absence of such parts. The heart differs vastly in form and function from the lungs, but both are essential to the health of a single body. So, too, the body of Torah. It consists of systems which in unison keep the world running. Torah sages are those internal organs through which G–d—the brain, the soul of it all—gives the world what it needs. If they disagree, it is not a disproof that G–d speaks through them. G–d causes one sage to emphasize one approach and another to emphasize another approach. Both are integral parts in the overall operation of the whole.

Nowadays, as the generations move further and further away from the time of the prophets, we have become more and more fragmented. Divisiveness amongst even those who uphold all the Principles of Faith is as pronounced as ever. Nevertheless, the Torah speaks even to our generation, and it speaks through the many leaders, each of whom represents *daas Torah* for his group. A Sephardic Jew goes to a Sephardic sage, an Ashkenazic Jew to an Ashkenazic sage, a Chassid to a Chassidic sage, etc.

Of course, even the greatest sage today is not on the level of the prophets. Still and all, Torah is our spiritual nourishment, and it is not possible to exist as a Jew without ingesting a regular diet of Torah as taught by its living sages. That is vital to remember whenever you meditate on this Principle. You cannot be spiritually alive without connection to living Torah sages.

How does one identify such a sage? I will relate advice a great person gave in his will to his children. The children themselves were accomplished scholars. Nevertheless, he told them, "Travel away from your home at least once a year to spend *Shabbos* by a *tzaddik*. How do you know who is a *tzaddik*? There are two criteria: they are elderly and they have disciples whom they have instilled with fear of heaven."

Thus, two credentials automatically qualify a *tzaddik*. He is an elderly person with an impressive track record of accomplishments. And his greatest accomplishment is that he molded disciples who possess fear of heaven. He is a teacher par excellence.

And one of the credentials without the other does not suffice. A great teacher who is nevertheless still young has not yet proven himself over the long run. Conversely, an eighty-year old holy man who performs wonders, but who did not achieve recognition for raising worthy disciples is also not assuredly the type of person who is a true mouthpiece for Torah. A true *tzaddik* needs age and accomplishment; he needs to have a proven track record of grooming others for greatness.

Let me reiterate that the above is not the simple understanding of the Rambam's sixth Principle, but merely

The Message

my way of bringing it home to us. The simple understanding is that the words of the prophets are true. G–d spoke to them knowing they would faithfully relay His thoughts and words for all generations. Nevertheless, included in the idea is the corollary principle of *daas Torah*, that G–d gave the Torah intending full well that it be interpreted by the true leaders of each generation, for all generations.

Moshe Rabbenu

The next Principle is closely tied to the previous one. In fact, we have to ask ourselves why it needs to be a separate Principle:

> "I believe with perfect faith that the prophecy of Moshe our teacher was absolutely true. He was the father of all prophets, those who came before him and those who arose after him."[1]

Since the Rambam includes this as a separate Principle, it is not enough to believe merely that the words of all the prophets are true. One has to believe that there is something special regarding Moshe's prophecy. What is it?

To answer that, first understand that there existed many more than the official forty-eight prophets and seven prophetesses whose prophecies are mentioned in

---

[1] See *Menachos* 29b. We have discussed this theme in *Self-Esteem*, the essay on *Shavuos*, subsection "Moshe and Rebbi Akiva."

the Torah. At least twice the amount of men who went out of Egypt, which translates into well over one million prophets, prophesied throughout the centuries in the land of Israel.

I like to compare prophecy to a radio broadcast. A prophet was someone who had the spiritual antenna to pick up the "prophecy" waves. The difference between the millions of prophets and the forty-eight recorded in *Tanach* was that the former had no license to disseminate to others what they heard G–d say.[1] They heard the "broadcast," but they themselves were not licensed to broadcast it to others. A false prophet therefore is not only someone who says false prophecy, but even someone who says true prophecy yet who has no permission to communicate it to others.[2]

Prophecy entails establishing a direct connection to G–d. However, there are different levels and degrees of connection. Moshe had a categorically greater connection than any other prophet. Other prophets spoke to G–d, but only with prior preparation. Moshe spoke to G–d day or night whenever he wanted to. Other prophets had what can be described as an almost epileptic fit when receiving prophecy. Moshe spoke to G–d with all his faculties intact, "face to face." However, the unique characteristic of Moshe's prophecy goes beyond those particulars.

---

[1] Even to our day it is possible that there are people worthy of receiving certain low-level transmissions from G–d, but have no permission to communicate it to others.

[2] Chasam Sofer.

The Message

Every prophet had a unique message. No two prophets conveyed the same directive. In sum, however, each of their messages resulted in one comprehensive, yet unified message. Moshe's message, though, was not just another particular, but the whole message itself.

To illustrate, picture the following. Sunshine is streaming into a room. You see the sunshine from your position in the room, but you do not see the actual sun. Moreover, your room has red windows, but your friend's room has blue windows. Another person has green windows, another's yellow, and so on. Everyone receives the sunshine, but only in the shade his particular room's window is colored.

A prophet was an exalted human being. Nevertheless, each prophet's perception was shaded by his particular individual nature. Moshe's perception was not so. His nature was literally universal. It was not influenced by personal idiosyncrasies and desires. He had nullified his personal coloration totally. To use the illustration above, his window was transparent. Moshe's message was not dependent on certain situations or eras. Everything was included in his prophecy because his connection to G–d was unclouded. He saw the sunlight directly, unfiltered.

Because his connection was so unique, only he is called "our teacher" (Moshe *Rabbenu*). And that means that each of us who can honestly call him "our teacher" has a direct connection to Moshe. He is behind everything we do. That is a powerful thought to reflect upon. When we make ourselves extensions of his teachings—when we live the Torah of Moshe—we become much more than individuals doing our own thing. We ourselves benefit from an undiluted light bestowed on the only human being in the history of the world who spoke to G–d "face to face." Consequently, our starting point is infinitely higher than anyone else who claims to be on a path to G–d. This is an extremely powerful idea.

Belief And Biblical Criticism

The above Principle, that G–d speaks to exalted human beings, sets up the next two Principles. Principle Eight reads:

> "I believe with perfect faith that the Torah which we have today in our hands is the actual Torah given to Moshe our teacher."

There was a time, not long ago, when it was much more difficult to have "perfect" faith in this Principle. Until the nineteenth century, the veracity of the Torah tradition was unquestioned. Then a new breed of "scholar" came into existence: the Bible Critic. With little or no proof, such critics arrogantly made claims that the stories of the Torah were fabrications. And because they were considered "intellectuals" in prestigious universities their claims were accepted as fact by many, many people even though they were made in the absence of archaeological evidence.

Then archaeologists began digging.

The Message

By the early 1900s, the evidence started mounting and it was becoming obvious that the Torah was accurate, down to the most minute background details. Consequently, the next generation of biblical historians, like renowned Professor W. F. Albright, had to admit: "Until recently, it was the fashion among biblical historians to treat the patriarchal sages of Genesis as though they were artificial creations of Israelite scribes of the divided monarchy, or possibly, tales told by imaginative story-tellers around Israelite campfires during the centuries following their occupation of the country. Eminent names among scholars can be cited for regarding every item from Genesis... as reflecting late inventions.... However, archaeological discoveries since 1925 have changed all this. Aside from a few diehards among older scholars, there is scarcely a single biblical historian who has not been impressed by the rapid accumulation of data supporting the substantial historicity of patriarchal tradition... There is no serious Bible scholar remaining who can argue with the fact of these historical events."

Another historian writes,[1] "Each passing year adds to our store of knowledge and provides us with more and more documents, inscriptions, monuments, and excavations which confirm its historical accuracy... Science is now in a position to state categorically that the Bible is factual till proven otherwise."

So much for the early Bible Critics.

---

[1] Will Durant, in *Story of Civilization*, Volume 1.

Beyond Survival

The truth is that the evidence goes beyond merely the written Torah. For 2,000 years, Jews have been scattered across the globe, yet even isolated Jewish communities such as those in Yemen have the exact same Torah, *tefillin*, and *mezuzos*. And this despite the fact that a single *mezuzah* requires compliance with approximately 5,000 detailed laws in order to be fit, while *tefillin* requires compliance with 30,000 laws, and a Torah scroll—over one million! And those laws are only known through the oral tradition. The Dead Sea Scrolls, too, prove that our *mesorah*, our traditions today, are letter for letter, detail for detail, as they always have been.

It is not our purpose here to pursue archaeological evidence fully.[1] And the truth is that our faith is not dependent at all upon archaeology. We know as a Principle of Faith that the "Torah which we have in our hands today is the actual Torah given to Moshe our teacher." Archaeological and scientific "facts" have proven fickle. Only Torah is immutable. We do not rely on man-made rationales or sciences. Nevertheless, it is nice to know that our belief has been vindicated—and by the very disciples of those who sought to discredit us! Now, more than ever we can say that our faith is complete, that "the Torah which we have in our hands today is the actual Torah given to Moshe our teacher."

---

[1] Neither have we even touched upon other fields turning up evidence, such as the scientifically rigorous work of Professor D. Witsum on the codes of the Torah. (See the essay, "Back to the Future," in the Appendix of *Choose Life!* for a concise description of the codes.)

The Message

Nothing New Under The Sun

The next Principle extends the belief that our tradition is intact:

"I believe with perfect faith that the Torah will never be changed and there will never be any other Torah given by the Creator."

Not only is the Torah which we have today the same as it always has been, but it will always remain that way. It will never be changed.

And it has to be that way. Torah is the blueprint of the world. "G–d looked into the Torah and created the world."[1] Consider the implications of that statement. Take, for instance, the commandment "Thou shalt not steal." If that idea existed before the world came into existence, before human beings existed, then when it came time for G–d to create the world, He must have, so to speak, asked, "What kind of world does the Torah need? If the Torah says, 'Do not steal,' then I have to make a world of people who want to steal."

It may sound strange, but think about it. If G–d wanted, He could have created a world where human nature was perfect, where no one wanted to steal. If you put a monkey at a table with a plate of money, will he steal it? No. Put a banana in the plate, though, and he will. G–d did not give the monkey the need to steal money, and He did not have to give it to human beings. But He

---

[1] *Beraishis Rabbah* 1:1.

did. And the reason is so that we would have the opportunity to use our free will in aligning ourselves with values in the Torah, values that are literally above this world.[1]

Torah is *not* for the sake of correcting human nature (although that is one of the goals toward which we strive). Human nature was created deficient in order to fulfill the Torah! Consequently, the Torah can never change. Human beings, if they want to achieve their own perfection, need to change in accordance with Torah. The Torah is not merely something created to fit human needs. Human needs were created to fit the Torah.

This concept is very important to believe with perfect faith because we do not know how we may be tested at any given time. If there should arise a person who the entire world says is the greatest human being; who performs miracles day and night; who is a great scholar; who meets all the credentials of a holy person, a prophet, etc.—and that person says, "I have a message from G‑d that you are allowed to eat pork from now on," he is a false prophet. The Torah will never be changed or exchanged.

And that scenario is not so far-fetched. Shabbatai Tzvi lived just over 300 years ago. He was an accomplished kabbalist who drew to his movement masses of people, including many very learned rabbis. Only those people who were able to detect some relatively minute changes

---

[1] And the same is true with all bad character traits. They were made and given to us precisely so that we should work to uproot them.

The Message

in Shabbatai Tzvi's Torah were not fooled. However, the tragedy of Shabbatai Tzvi destroyed untold numbers of lives before the saga played itself out. Therefore, your life may one day literally depend on the depth with which you believe that the Torah will never be changed.

Is there no room for creativity, then? Haven't great scholars throughout the generations produced original works? Didn't they innovate new ideas which never had been known previously?

The Talmud states that, "Any innovation which a true disciple innovates was known to Moshe." Moshe was the most transparent receiver of information, as we explained. He saw everything clearly. After him, information was received by way of tradition to many sages and prophets. Nevertheless, everything they received was contained in Moshe's original conception. Even today, any wondrously sounding true, innovative Torah idea had previously been known to Moshe on Mount Sinai. There is room for innovation and creativity then, but it must ultimately be rooted in the unchangeable Torah of Moshe.

The Torah cannot be changed. Once a responsible person understands this, not only is innovation allowed but it is encouraged. The Zohar states that G–d celebrates whenever we innovate "new" Torah thoughts. He is joyful whenever we discover a new insight, a new application of *halacha*, etc. Why? Because whenever we make a discovery which previously had only been known 3,300 years ago by Moshe we awaken a spark of the revelation at Sinai. We are transported from our present time and place back 3,300 years. G–d rejoices because He sees that His children are still under the wedding canopy of Mount Sinai.

"There is nothing new under the sun." Nevertheless, the Zohar adds, ". . . that which is above the sun can be new." When we transport ourselves back to Sinai, back to Moshe our teacher, we connect to the undiluted light of Torah. In so doing, we reach back into the original source of renewal and rejuvenation. That original revelation—a revelation emanating from above the sun—is infinite and filled with never-ending possibilities of discovery.

Chapter 6

Justice

CHAPTER 6

Justice

Principle 10: "I believe with perfect faith that the Creator knows all the deeds and all the thoughts of every human being, as it is written, *He has fashioned every heart; He pays attention to all their deeds.*"

Principle 11: "I believe with perfect faith that the Creator rewards those who keep His commandments, and punishes those who violate His commandments."

Before even beginning an analysis of the tenth Principle, a superficial reading of it should give us a tremendous boost of self-confidence. When you see ants scurrying about on the ground do they really warrant your attention? Who cares what "epic" ant-battles are won or lost? If so, what then are we to the Creator of the universe? Not even ants. Why then should He care about what we do or think?

However, not only does G–d pay attention to all our deeds, but He cares about our thoughts. He knows what you ate for breakfast and how you enjoyed it. Therefore, the very idea that G–d knows our deeds and thoughts should fill us with tremendous self-confidence and self-worth. I am a very important being. The Creator of the universe cares about what I do and think. I am a somebody. Nobody is a nobody.

Now, the fact that this, the tenth Principle, exhorts us to have faith that G–d knows our thoughts and deeds seems redundant. We said in the first Principle that G–d created us and continues to recreate us every second, perpetually invigorating us with new vitality and life. Should He stop for a moment we would cease to exist. Why then is it necessary to emphasize that He knows all the deeds and thoughts of every human being? If we have existence this moment only because He actively wills it, then of course He knows not only our deeds, both public and private, but even the content of our thoughts.

The answer is that the special emphasis of this Principle is that our thoughts are just as important as our deeds. *Who we are on the inside is as important (and in some ways more important) as who we are on the outside.* We are not free to think whatever we wish to think. It is not enough to perform good deeds with our bodies while our minds are immersed in the muck of the street.

And that should give us all pause. Imagine that scientists could invent a camera which recorded all your thoughts. Would you allow yourself to be recorded for public display even for just one hour? I have yet to meet the person who has told me sincerely that he or she would accept such an offer. Yet, G–d has such a "camera"

Justice

which registers and records our thoughts no less than it registers and records our deeds. "Who testifies about us in the hereafter? . . . Your own soul."[1] The mind is a running videotape. Every experience and word, as well as every thought is permanently recorded on our mind's film. We cannot escape this fact.

Of course, the fact that G–d knows our thoughts works to our benefit, as well. If He knows my thoughts, then He knows my highest aspirations. After all, our dreams, hopes, and desires always far exceed our actions. If G–d knows me by my thoughts, then He knows my best self. He knows I want to be Moshe, even though that is not who I am. He knows I am better than I act. That is to my benefit.

"He knows all the deeds and all the thoughts of every human being." That is a statement which should give us great confidence and relief, and yet great pause. The two go hand in hand. We cannot benefit from the awareness that G–d cares about us and knows our true goodness unless we simultaneously admit that we can be held responsible for what we do and even for what we think.

He Who Fashions The Heart Is Just

The verse brought in support of this Principle reads, "He has fashioned every heart; He pays attention to all their deeds." What does it mean to say that G–d *fashions every heart*? Wouldn't we expect it to say, He *pays*

---

[1] *Taanis* 11a.

attention to the thoughts of every heart (just as it says, He *pays attention* to our deeds)? What is the deeper implication of saying He "fashions" every heart?

We live in a world of falsehood (*almah d'shikrah*). There is no escaping the negative influences of our environment. Sometimes bad or illusory thoughts that we would never conjure up ourselves enter our minds from outside sources. How then can we be responsible for such thoughts?

The answer is that we are responsible *if we cultivate them*. We do not have to be the cause of the thought, but if once it is there we cultivate it, like a farmer cultivates a seed, we become responsible for it. And we cultivate bad thoughts in three ways: meditating on them, verbalizing them, and acting upon them. Each level (thought, speech, action) engenders a level of culpability that would have been avoided if the thought would have simply been ignored at its first occurrence.

The question is: Is it fair of G–d to challenge us with negative thoughts brought on by outside influences? Wouldn't it have been fairer if we just had to be responsible our own thoughts? G–d could have created each of us on his own planet. Why did He have to put us in a world where negative influences come upon us through no choice of our own?

Obviously, then, G–d put us in a world of influences for a purpose. Each negative thought or influence that comes our way is our *tikkun*, a specially designed challenge which only we were meant to overcome. And when

Justice

we overcome it we are better off than had we not been so challenged. Admittedly, the challenge of pushing away bad thoughts is difficult and frustrating—especially at the beginning. Nevertheless, persistence will pay off. Little by little we learn to not preoccupy ourselves with those negative thoughts. Finally, it as if they never even entered our minds.

Of course, no matter how much we try, a particularly nagging thought can persistently "pop up" in our minds over and over again for an entire lifetime, and perhaps even during the last moments of our life. Nevertheless, the idea is to avoid becoming obsessed with such thoughts, and to recognize that each negative thought is our personal area of responsibility in this life. We were put here to continually disassociate ourselves from it until our dying day. That is the *tikkun* (literally, repair) we were put on this earth to effect.

This point requires further elaboration.

The first step in the process of making jewelry is creating the model. The model is then dipped into a soft plaster-of-paris type mold which eventually hardens into a negative impression of the jewelry. A perceptive individual can look at the impression and already see how the piece of jewelry will look. Obviously, the more deeply sunk into the mold an impression is, the more expensive the piece of jewelry it will produce.

People are created with certain natures. "Nature" in Hebrew, *tevah*, is related to *t'viah*, "sunk in." Through understanding the deficiencies—the *t'viah*, the part that is sunk in, the hollow mold—you can come to know your ideal self. A person has low self-esteem because he believes he is a nothing. He sees himself and he sees a void. However, every negative characteristic we have in ourselves reveals our potential greatness. The greater the void, the greater the amount of substance which can be filled into that void. A human being is placed in this world to fill deficiencies. How much can a person accomplish? It depends upon how many deficiencies he has been granted, on how "sunk in" his nature is.

Imagine a new technology which could turn ordinary material into diamonds, and that there were several types of machines to perform this task. One machine could turn gold into diamonds. Another could turn silver into diamonds. A third could turn copper into diamonds. And, finally, one machine could convert garbage into diamonds. Which machine would you buy? Obviously, the last machine. Even if the initial cost was much higher than the other machines, there is so much garbage in the world—free garbage—you would never lack raw material to produce diamonds.

That is what G–d does for us. Our bad life's circumstances, our undesirable character traits, our physical urges, our bad thoughts, etc. are the garbage. If it were up to us, we would throw the garbage out, but G–d does not let us do so. He delivers unwanted raw material to our doorstep every day. So many people to whom I talk tell me, "I had a terrible upbringing," or, "I had terrible influences," or, a "I had a terrible marriage," or, "I have

Justice

no self-control," etc. What are they complaining about? Our garbage is a reflection of our potential; it is our raw material. The more garbage, the more raw material we have to be transformed into diamonds.

Of course, it is not comfortable to work with garbage. The machine may take seven or eight years before it turns the garbage into diamonds. A person could very well say, "I don't want to work in garbage for seven or eight years." However, that is short-sighted. When all you see is the garbage, of course you do not want it. However, when you can envision the final outcome you can be patient while the process of transformation is going on.

Sometimes, the process does not take just seven or eight years, but seventy or eighty years. Still, regarding spiritual diamonds, what is seventy or eighty years compared to eternity?

To say that G–d shortchanged you by giving you so many personal deficiencies without the concomitant ability to transform them into advantages is to accuse Him of not knowing what He is doing. G–d knows what He is doing! We must always remember that. He molded our souls and saw what each of us could accomplish. Then He placed us in a world where we have those exact deficiencies necessary to bring out our highest potential. We must have as much faith in ourselves as He has in us.

Given this overview, we can now see how all the bad influences to which we have been exposed are part of the larger plan designed by G–d. And that is what it means

Beyond Survival

"He *fashions* every heart." He does not merely pay attention to each heart. He *designed* it even before we knew about it. He knows about all our difficulties better than we do. He fashioned them all. Each challenge is a perfect fit. It is perfectly just, calculated down to the smallest detail to be in exact accord with precisely what we need to correct in ourselves in order to become whole.

Understand this very crucial point. There is no person alive who has not been born into some situation of misfortune that is beyond his or her control. One person has no home life. Another has no money. Some have no self-control. And so on. Each person at his or her root is innocent of causing the problems which so overwhelm him or her. Each is truly a victim of circumstance.

Nevertheless, even if you can disclaim responsibility for your shortcomings—after all, "G–d [not you or your parents ultimately] fashions every heart"—yet, "He pays attention to all their deeds." You are never relieved of the responsibility to work through your major problems no matter what. Each of us was sent down to this world into a different setting, solely by G–d, but He gave us the free will to react to our situation for good or bad. We are entitled to fail. However, we are not entitled to make excuses to the point where we resign ourselves to a permanent state of failure. We are not entitled to quit.

"But I've tried," you say.

"Keep on trying."

"But I've tried over and over again."

"Then try a new approach. Change your strategy."

Justice

"Still, no matter how many times I've tried, or how many different ways I've tried, nothing seems to work."

"Even if that's true, it is not your obligation to succeed. It is your obligation to *try* to succeed. You must attempt to overcome each problem even if each time you push the problem away it returns. A problem may plague you until you are old and frail. Still, you are not freed of the obligation to try. *Success is not defined by having the problem one day vanish. Success is defined by how much you continually put forth effort which can potentially overcome the problem.* The problem itself can ultimately only be resolved by He who fashions every heart. You must measure your success by how much effort you put forth toward overcoming the problem."

We have been placed in a world of separation. We are separated from G–d, and the world continually pulls us further away. Sin creates even more distance. Nevertheless, the primary goal of every human being is to return to G–d, to end the state of separation. And the greater the original distance, the greater the impact of reunion. G–d fashions those hearts which He knows have the greatest potential, together with those positions in life where one begins furthest removed from the goal. The ultimate goal is, though, to remember that we have a responsibility to do *teshuva*, to try to correct our deficiencies. The bottom line is that the separation is G–d's doing, but the ultimate closeness is dependent upon our doing.

Reward And Punishment

Given that the Creator knows all our deeds and thoughts—all our legitimate excuses and all our illegitimate ones—the eleventh Principle follows naturally:

"I believe with perfect faith that the Creator rewards those who keep His commandments, and punishes those who violate His commandments."

G–d does not want to punish us. He created us to bestow upon us reward. However, sometimes for the sake of ultimate reward, discipline is best called for. Yet, even when it is, it is not a punishment, but a corrective measure designed to somehow help us improve.[1] When a person abuses free will and chooses bad, evil results. However, that in itself can be the trigger for rechoosing good. Evil is a symptom; it is a natural result of using free will to choose bad. Like the physical sensation of pain or pangs of hunger, it signals us that somewhere along the line something is wrong—somewhere we chose bad over good. And then, like pain, that very evil motivates us to seek a cure and to rechoose good over bad.

"In the place where a *baal teshuva* stands, even a completely righteous person cannot stand." A *baal teshuva* is someone who overcame evil and adversity to "return" to the way of G–d. And, as many of today's "returnees" attest, it was the very adversity which motivated them to return in the first place. I like to compare it to a hose. If

---

[1] Deuteronomy 8:5.

Justice

you want the water in a typical garden hose to reach far, two contradictory forces are needed. First, you need a high amount of water pressure, and second you need a nozzle which limits the water from exiting the hose. A large supply of water with a large opening will not send the water far. Similarly, a very small opening with a small amount of water pressure will not spray the water far either. In order for our actions to reach far, two forces are needed: a great surge for good and a great limitation on that good.

In my own experience, I have seen this concept borne out time and again. In two or three years, people from the most alienated backgrounds became bursting wells of Torah knowledge and character; people capable of building other people, and even entire communities. "In the place where a *baal teshuva* stands, even a completely righteous person cannot stand." The completely righteous may have a powerful flow, but they do not have the same nozzle. The more restrictive the nozzle, the further the water goes (once enough of a surge is mustered).

Reward and punishment in this world are usually not what they seem to be. A person in a coma has everything done for him. People dress him, undress him, wash him, feed him, observe him, treat him, etc. He is taken care of completely. The more helpless a person is, the more he is taken care of. The stronger a person is, on the other hand, the less he is taken care of. G-d works with us in the same way. When we are helpless, He takes special care of us. When we are strong, He seemingly withdraws—but that is generally only in order to give us the opportunity to succeed on our own. Ease can be a sign of bad; difficulty, a sign of favor. Free will is always balanced for our ultimate good.

"Punishment," then, in the form of evil which comes upon a person, is never without its calculation. It is generally part of G–d's plan to spark the person to an ever new discovery of his true inner goodness. As such, it cannot really be called punishment in the way many people understand the term, i.e. retribution. G–d continually weighs the scales, balancing our world, giving exactly what we need for our ultimate good until our very last breath.

Nevertheless, ". . . the Creator rewards those who keep His commandments, and punishes those who violate His commandments." Every individual will ultimately receive the just deserts of his actions. But, by then he will have nothing to complain about. He will be shown how people with deficiencies—people burdened with suffering and surrounded by evil—transformed their handicaps into diamonds. He will be shown their life and he will have to admit to the justice of his verdict.[1]

Obviously, that is a very frightening thought to ponder. However, ". . . those who keep His commandments" can look forward to reward. People reap what they sow. Our life in the next world will be a direct reflection of our life in this world.

Let me crystallize that thought with a parable.

---

[1] *Taanis* 11a.

Justice

A person prayed to be shown the afterlife and had his request granted. First, he was taken to *Gehinnom* (the place of punishment in the afterlife). To his surprise, he was led into a magnificent banquet hall filled with every delicacy imaginable, all exquisitely and temptingly prepared. Just the aroma of the hot, steaming food was enough to make the stomach growl. The regal banquet hall was filled with well-dressed people sitting at the tables.

As the visitor continued his "tour," he noticed that the people inside were grimacing. It looked as if they were starving. Then he noticed that although the food was laid out in front of them they were not eating. "Why aren't they eating?" he thought.

He took a second look and noticed that there was something very strange about the eating utensils. They were at least two or three feet long! Then he was told that the rule was that the food could only be eaten with these utensils. Everyone had food on the end of his fork, but no one could put it into his mouth. They just could not feed themselves no matter how they tried. Thus, even though everything was available—and temptingly so—they were starving. That was *Gehinnom*.

The visitor was then taken to Paradise. To his utter shock he was led into a banquet hall set up in the exact same fashion! Exquisite, tempting food, well-dressed people, and even the same three-foot utensils. Everything seemed exactly the same—except that each person in this banquet hall had a look of satisfaction on his face.

Beyond Survival

Indeed, here the people were eating. "But how can they eat," he thought, "if they have only the same long utensils and the same rule that they must eat using these utensils?" Then, he took a second look and understood the solution. Each person was feeding his neighbor across the table. That was Paradise.

Why couldn't the first group figure out the same problem and feed each other? Because in this world they only learned how to take. During life they never trained themselves to give, and in the next life they have no opportunity to train themselves in new ways.

The next world is one. However, the experiences of its inhabitants are two. There is an abundant availability of the most satisfying spiritual delicacies in the afterlife. Nevertheless, one will be satisfied in the next world only to the degree he learned to become a giver in this world.

My point is that we are the creators of our afterlife. There is a direct correlation to what a person does in this world and the way that person will experience the next world. You make your own *Gehinnom*. You make your own Paradise. There is one reality: the ever-presence of G–d. But there are many different experiences. A person experiences satisfaction in the next world according to the tools of being which he developed—or failed to develop—in life.

Chapter 7

The Coming Of The Messiah

CHAPTER 7

The Coming of the Messiah

Principle 12: "I believe with perfect faith in the coming of the Messiah, and though he may tarry—nevertheless I wait for him each day."

We opened this book by explaining that the characteristic which distinguishes the Principles of Faith from other concepts, vital though they may be, is that the Principles of Faith have far-ranging, all-encompassing effects on *all* our actions in our everyday lives. To draw a comparison, the global effect on a person who lacks faith in the previous Principle, the Principle of reward and punishment, is easily measured. One who thinks his actions carry no consequences will behave far differently in all areas of life than one who knows that every act is scrutinized. And the same is true with all the other Principles.

Now, suppose one is a good person who serves G–d in every way, except he feels disconnected from the entire

Beyond Survival

issue of the Messiah (*Mashiach*). Will that really effect his life? When he comes, he comes. What difference, really, does it make now that we *believe* in his coming?

And the question is even stronger because the wording of this Principle emphasizes the need to be continually aware of *Mashiach*. For example, we are waiting for his "coming," i.e. we are *not* waiting for him to be here in the future, for him "to come." His coming is a happening now, in the present tense. Furthermore, the fact that we have to look forward to his coming ". . . no matter how long he may tarry" means that we still have to keep his hopeful arrival on our minds no matter how dismal things appear.[1] And, finally, the concluding words state that we are to wait for him ". . . each day." Not only can this be understood to mean that we are to wait for him *every* day, but *all* day (*b'chall yom*) as well; i.e.. we are not supposed to let a moment of our day pass without waiting for him. Thus, it is clear that it is very important for us to always be ready to expect his arrival. The question

---

[1] Actually, when things are most dismal that is when we most need *Mashiach*. In the last weeks before the end of the Second World War, when my family and I were hiding out and starving in war-torn Europe, we were sure *Mashiach's* arrival was imminent. During the Gulf War, people were talking about observing *Pesach* with *Mashiach*. Despair breeds such yearnings. The fact is that it is harder to believe in his coming when the situation is not so desperate. And thus, in many ways, such complacency is the greatest situation of desperation. It puts us into a feeling of false security when we would not naturally long for *Mashiach*. This, I like to explain, is the real meaning of "even though he may tarry," i.e. even when I am least likely to expect his coming—when things are going well—even then I must wait longingly for him.

The Coming Of The Messiah

is, what benefit does this state of readiness produce for our present life? What, really, do we gain in our daily lives by waiting for *Mashiach*?

The Maharal offers an insight which can help us answer the question. He explains that every person is a kind of miniature *Mashiach*. We each have a piece of him in us—at least in potential. However, in order to activate that potential we must at least first know what *Mashiach's* coming is going to give us.

The prophet tells us that the era of *Mashiach* is the time when ". . . the earth will be filled with the knowledge of G–d as the waters cover the sea."[1] Knowledge of G–d is the root of an individual's mental (and of course spiritual) health. If we know G–d exists, then we have the means to handle all our problems. After all, nothing is more demoralizing and unhealthy than the belief that one bears a heavy burden in vain. Conversely, there is no greater comfort than to know that our suffering is not pointless. As long as we know that our pain will one day bear fruit, we do not even have to necessarily know exactly what that fruit will be. All we need to maintain a healthy frame of mind is to know that G–d has a purpose in everything that happens to us. Therefore, the more true knowledge of G–d we possess, the more armed we are to confront life's challenges.

And that is why understanding the meaning of *Mashiach* is so vital. *Mashiach* is very frequently mentioned in connection with suffering and tragedy. He is

---

[1] Isaiah 11:9.

Beyond Survival

called the "son of David," because no one was confronted with trial and tribulation like David, to which *Tehillim* (the Book of Psalms) attests. *Mashiach* is also described as sitting by the gates of Rome, perpetually bandaging and unbandaging himself.[1] (Rome is the paradigm of exile and bandages are symbolic of suffering.) He is similarly called "son of the fallen one" (*bar-nafli*).[2] *Mashiach* represents human resiliency; the capacity to stand up after a fall; to withstand suffering and ultimately rise to greatness from it. *And the secret of Mashiach's resiliency is his unparalleled connection to G–d.* As long as he keeps in the forefront of his mind that G–d is his shepherd, then he can confront any suffering—he can even walk through the valley of the shadow of death and fear no evil. Thus, it is *Mashiach's* intractable knowledge of G–d which gives him the wherewithal to persevere and overcome.

The era ushered in by *Mashiach* will bear his stamp. All humanity will be filled with the knowledge of G–d. It is an era in which the reason for all past sufferings will become perfectly clear. Compare it to a mystery movie. A mystery movie is designed to keep the viewers in suspense; to keep them afraid, confused, on the edge of their seats, and even in tears—all so that in the last five minutes everything will become perfectly clear. History, as we know it, is the supreme mystery movie. Its entire purpose is to keep us confused and in suspense. And, then, toward the very end, *Mashiach* arrives and everything

---

[1] *Sanhedrin* 98a.
[2] Ibid. 96b.

The Coming Of The Messiah

suddenly makes perfect sense. Only at the end do all the parts fit in place.[1]

Mashiach will fill the world with knowledge. However, his coming must first be paved by our actions. We must first begin filling the world with the knowledge of G–d. How do we do that? Each of us is like a light bulb. ("The soul of man is a candle of G–d."[2]) Some of us give off ten watts, some twenty watts, some fifty watts, some one hundred watts, etc. Whatever our "wattage," though, each of us was assigned to generate a certain degree of light (i.e. knowledge of G–d) into this world. *Mashiach* will come when our light, combined with every one else's light, will reach a predesignated level; a level called "the great light"—which is the knowledge of G–d representative of the era of *Mashiach*.

That light—our light—is the contribution to "the great light" which will cover the entire earth with the knowledge of G–d. We are partners, then, working on one great project to light up the world. And our partnership extends back to our parents and grandparents, and their parents and grandparents, all the way back to Abraham, who was the first person to generate the one great light. Of course, Abraham's light may be a million kilowatt generator compared to my five watt bulb, but *Mashiach* cannot come until my little contribution is made. My light, my parents' light, and all my ancestors'

---

[1] "A song of ascents: When G–d will return the captivity of *Tzion* we will be like dreamers; then our mouth will be filled with laughter and our tongue with song." (*Tehillim* 126)

[2] Proverbs 20:27.

Beyond Survival

light, etc.—no matter how big or small—all must shine in their own time and in their own way in order to produce the era of *Mashiach*. Before then *Mashiach* cannot come.

Thus, each of us has a portion of *Mashiach* in ourselves. We activate it when we develop an ever deepening connection to G-d. And there is no greater opportunity to develop that connection than during our most challenging life circumstances.[1] However, we cannot even

---

[1] As mentioned above, the verse states, "The soul of man is a candle of G-d." The Zohar elaborates on the symbolism of the candle (or, more accurately, the oil lamp). Our body is like the wick. Our soul is the flame. And our life—as expressed in good deeds—is the oil. Now, oil is produced by squeezing and crushing the olive. So, too, when our lives are most crushed and challenged we produce the most oil (i.e. life). Thus, it is the difficulties in life (the oil) which determines the flame, which produces the light we shine into this world.

We are not responsible for the amount of light we shine, for that is up to G-d. G-d had a unique design in mind for each of us before we were even born, and He set aside the precise amount of "olives" (i.e. life challenges) for us. We have no choice in that. And, indeed, many of life's real difficulties are beyond our control. Our choice lies in how we react to such difficulties. We have the choice what we do with the olive, namely: to eat it or crush it. Life and its inevitable difficulties can be ignored; we can tranquilize the pain in many ways, including immersing ourselves in one distracting form of entertainment after another to outright denying there is an ultimate reason for the suffering. In any event, to avoid our pain is to "eat up" or discard our "olives."

I am not advocating masochism or martyrdom. We should seek to alleviate our pain and correct it at its source. However, while we experience it we must not be afraid to confront its meaning head on. Our life's difficulties—and they are "ours," designed specially for us—were meant to spur us to greater spiritual heights; ultimately to set up a communication link with G-d. Doing so, turns our "olives" into "oil." Our suffering becomes redemption. Our failures become successes. Our lives, light.

The Coming Of The Messiah

begin to activate any of it if we are not waiting for *Mashiach,* if we do not know what his coming is intended to give us. His coming is intended to fill the world with the knowledge of G-d. He can only shine his light on the whole world if we first light up our little corner of the world. When we do so, it is as if *Mashiach* is already here. We can feel his presence ". . . even though he may tarry."

Thus, there is not one second in life when it is not possible to produce this *Mashiach* quality. That is the deeper explanation which best reveals why believing in his coming is a far-ranging, all-encompassing Principle of Faith. Our entire purpose in life is to produce our pre-designated portion of *Mashiach,* i.e. the light of the knowledge of G-d. As long as we keep in the forefront of our minds that G-d is our shepherd, then we can confront any situation—tragic or ecstatic—and turn it into a great light. Therefore, being ever cognizant of the concept of *Mashiach* is vital to our everyday happiness and ability to persevere. There is no moment without its potential light. Every moment is another unique opportunity to contribute our unique light—a great light which the world waits to see shine. Is there a more inspiring and motivating thought to make part of your everyday consciousness?

The Teshuva Prophecy

Our Sages teach that we will be redeemed through *teshuva*, through sincere "return" to the ways and values of the Torah. The idea is that it is not enough to just have *Mashiach* come, but to be prepared for his coming. We must do *teshuva* first. This leads us to one of the most profound and pertinent predictions in the Torah,[1] the prediction of the Jewish Peoples' *teshuva* ("return") in the End of Days. The classic commentators discern four levels or stages of *teshuva* which will precede his coming. Let us examine each of these four stages individually.

> And it will be that when all these things come to pass—the blessing and the curse—which I have placed before you, then you will return to your heart, [from] in the midst of all the nations where G–d your G–d pushed you to. (Deut. 30:1)

In essence, this verse tells us that after all the good tidings and all the bad tidings—which were prophesied in the previous chapters of the Torah—come to pass, a wave of *teshuva* will sweep through the descendants of Israel. (The Ramban writes explicitly that this verse and the ensuing ones refer to the time preceding *Mashiach's* coming.)

From where will this return occur? From ". . . in the midst of the nations . . . ." The phrase refers to even more than just physically living in the middle of the nations. It refers to the spiritual state of being in the middle of the nations as well. Unfortunately, it is an all-too-well-known fact that an extremely high percentage of

---

[1] We have discussed the following in detail in *Days Are Coming*, especially Part I, Chapter 2.

The Coming Of The Messiah

cult members are Jews. How does a Jewish boy end up in an ashram or on a mountain in India? This is a fulfillment of the prophecy that we will be dispersed into "... the midst of the nations." Not only physically, but spiritually. And it does not only refer to Jews in cults, for any Jew whose lifestyle is an imitation of the non-Jew can be said to be living in the "... midst of the nations." Thus, the verse predicts that there will come a time when Jews will have tried every fad, philosophy, cult, etc.—and they will not just be participants, but they will become the leaders, the gurus, the Nobel Prize winners—and they will indulge themselves in everything the nations have to offer... everything, that is, except "their heart."[1]

---

[1] The verse says that we were exiled in the first place because "G-d pushed" us there. The understanding is that whatever "natural" political, societal, and military forces can be used to explain the exile, such forces were nothing more than instruments in the hand of G-d to achieve results that He, alone, decreed. It was only G-d, Himself, who dispersed us to the "four corners" of the earth.

Why would G-d do that? Why did He "push" us into "the midst of the nations"? The answer is, because from within that very self-alienation, we would return to our roots with a greater determination than ever. And "... you are going to do *teshuva* ... in the midst of all the nations." There will not be one off-the-wall ideology and idolatry in which Jews will not be found. Cults, cultural movements, countercultural movements, political movements, counter-political movements—you name it, Jews can be found there.

Yet, we have to know that G-d is the One who dispatched us into "... the midst of the nations." Why? Ultimately, in order to see through their shiny exterior—the allure of a new, man-made idealism—and reject it. Why the need to be cast into "the nations" and their ideologies merely in order to reject them? Because, in the end, that will help us to better appreciate what it is we have. In other words, by finding out what the endless array of man-made ideologies and cultures really lead to, we will eventually come to appreciate "our

Beyond Survival

Now, the Abarbanel, writing over 500 years ago, states that prior to *Mashiach*, the Jewish people will be divided into two groups: those who are totally assimilated—those ". . . in the midst of the nations," the majority—and those who keep the Torah and its *mitzvos*.[1] The former, he explains, are subsumed in this verse. It is the assimilated Jew who is specifically told, "You will return to your heart." He explains that to mean that it will *only be in their heart*; they will not be able to express it outwardly. It will be cooped up in their hearts. They will say, "Something doesn't feel right. Something is missing. I am not

---

heart" to a much greater degree.

[1] Rashi also draws this inference, but from a different source: "Distant ones, hear what I have done; close ones, know My might." (Isaiah 33:14) After drawing the inference, Rashi's elaboration on the verse is surprising. The verse mentions two types of Jews: distant ones and near ones. Given the alternatives, the average person would say that "the distant ones" are the Jews raised in an assimilated environment, while "the close ones" are Jews raised in an environment where Torah is observed. However, Rashi interprets as follows: "*The distant ones (rechokim)*, refers to the ones who believe in Me, and perform My will from their youth. *The near ones (k'rovim)*, refers to the *baalei teshuva* (the sincere returnees) who have come close to Me recently." In other words, the ones who are far are the ones who always kept the Torah. The ones who are close are the ones who only recently started keeping it. It is the exact opposite of what we would have thought!

The explanation is that Jews born into and raised in this unimaginably rich spiritual heritage called Torah can more easily have their spiritual sensitivities grow numb. On the other hand, a one-time alienated Jew, who comes back to Torah because he searched and toiled, is doubly wealthy. He has the wealth and he appreciates its value. "According to the pain, so is the reward." And, therefore, without *teshuva*, although he is a good Jew, a Jew observing the Torah for no other reason than that he has done so from his youth is not as close to G–d as the genuine *baal teshuva*.

The Coming Of The Messiah

satisfied with the way I am. My values, my life—it's all wrong; it's all superficial." That person will not yet admit or consider the possibility that keeping the Torah is the solution to his inner anguish and ambivalence. Nevertheless, something in his heart will gnaw at him. He knows that the ideologies (the contemporary world's idols) he had always pinned his hopes on are powerless.

Thus, the first of the four stages is that a simple spirit of *teshuva* will exist, although it will not necessarily be translated into practice.

The second stage is reported in the next verse.

> Then you will return up until G–d your G–d and listen to His voice, concerning everything that I commanded you this day—you and your children—with all your heart and with all your soul. (Deut. 30:2)

The commentary of the Sforno on this verse contains the following explanation:

> You will do *teshuva* ("you will *return*") purely for the sake of heaven, for the sake of G–d . . . not like people who do the commandments by rote, as you had been doing them prior to this time.

This second verse indicates a second type of Jew. While the first verse is centered on those who are ". . . in the midst of the nations," this verse makes no such mention. It refers to the *teshuva* of those already committed

Beyond Survival

to living a Jewish lifestyle, those who do the commandments, but not with the greatest enthusiasm. They will not essentially have to change the outer trappings; they will only have to deepen their Judaism; to carry out the Torah more fully, with more sincerity and inner joy.

This group will do *teshuva* in the manner of "... you and your children." The surest indicator of an authentic Judaism is when the children follow in their parents' footsteps. Children are very sensitive. If they see their parents missing a truly deep commitment or lacking a sense of joy in their Torah lifestyle they pick up on it. Thus, children who willingly follow in the path of their parents probably do so because they sensed that their parents were sincere; they felt that they were exposed to "the real thing," not a synthetic representation. Judaism which "... you *and your children*" keep is the kind of Judaism done "with all your heart and with all your soul."

This second type of Jew, then, never abandoned the body of Judaism. Nevertheless, he became robot-like performing his obligations. He slowly distanced himself from the inner richness of the Torah. He, too, has *teshuva* to do, as this verse indicates.

After he begins the *teshuva* process, then:

> ... G–d your G–d will return your returning, and have compassion on you, and return and gather you from all the nations which G–d your G–d scattered you to. (Deut. 30:3)

The Coming Of The Messiah

Mashiach waits for our initiative, as we said. And we will take that initiative one way or another, sooner or later. Will our *teshuva* occur in a long, slow, drawn out process, or will it occur overnight?[1] We do not know. But it will happen. At that point we will be a nation of people who have begun the *teshuva* process, but who have not necessarily completed it. And that leads to an important point. No matter how hard we try, we may not end up changing our natures. *Teshuva* is our initiative to bring about our own improvement—and it is our obligation to take that initiative—but nowhere is it guaranteed that our hard work must end in the revolution of our beings. Success is ultimately a gift from G-d. The same thoughts, the same doubts, the same habits, the same shortcomings, etc. can still plague us, as we said in the previous chapter, until our dying day, despite our best efforts. And yet that does not relieve us of the obligation to try.

Nevertheless, once the first two stages of *teshuva* have been satisfactorily performed—the assimilated Jew rediscovers his heart, and the outwardly committed Jew becomes an inwardly committed Jew—then the third stage of *teshuva* occurs: "G-d your G-d will return (*shav*) your returning (*sh'vuscha*)," which means that He will

---

[1] How can it happen "overnight"? Unfortunately, it is getting less and less difficult to envision. All we need is one madman to gain power and step in front of the United Nations and say, "The Jews are the cause of all our problems." It happened in Nazi Germany, amongst the most civilized culture of its day. It can, G-d forbid, happen again.

complete your *teshuva* (*shav* and *sh'vuscha* share the same root as *teshuva*). Your *teshuva* will start paying dividends, and the results of your efforts toward personal development will become manifest.

The prior three stages lead to the fourth level of *teshuva*:

> And G-d your G-d will circumcise your heart and the heart of your offspring—to love G-d your G-d with all your heart and with all your soul so that you may live. (Deut. 30:6)

Circumcising the heart, explains the Ramban, means killing the evil inclination (*yetzer hara*). That results in the highest level of attachment to, and ecstasy in G-d, which was the level Adam had in the Garden of Eden before he sinned. Before reaching that point, though, we as a nation will pass through the previous stages. It is upon each of us, then—be we Jews of the first type or second—to commit ourselves wholeheartedly to the standards of spiritual growth outlined in the Torah.

Chapter 8

Life Recycling Life

CHAPTER 8

Life Recycling Life

Principle 13: "I believe with perfect faith that the dead will be brought back to life when the Creator wills it,[1] and His memory will be elevated for ever and ever."

The belief that "... the dead will be brought back to life" does not address the idea that our *souls* live on forever,[2] which is obviously assumed, but that our *bodies* will be brought back to life in order to live on forever, too. This is a radical concept. For instance, the Eastern religions are known to emphasize how the essential person is only his soul, and clearly not his body. Thus, they define a holy person as one who meditates all day, fasts as much as he can, avoids intimate relationships, denies and defies all bodily pleasures (for example, by lying on a bed of

---

[1] Whereas we can speed along the process of bringing *Mashiach*, as we explained in the last chapter, we cannot change the time of the Resurrection of the Dead. It can only occur "when G–d wills it."
[2] See our chapter entitled *Oneness And The Soul*, which covers Principles 2,3,4.

nails), etc. For them the ultimate goal is achieved when a person totally dissociates himself from and rejects his body. For Torah, it is just the opposite. The ultimate will be when the body is reunited with the soul!

And the Torah's ideal begs the question: What is gained by saying our bodies will one day be brought back to life? What value, really, is there in physical life? An infant comes into this world, grows up, lives seventy or eighty years and dies. The average person weighs seven or eight pounds at birth and about 180 pounds at death. He lives, works, makes money, spends it, eats a lot of food in between, pollutes the world, creates other little polluters, etc., and in the end all he physically has to show for his lifetime of activity is a net gain of somewhere in the neighborhood of 172 pounds. Is it worth it? And if you calculate all the tons of food he had to eat in order to end up with only 172 pounds of net gain, it appears even less worth it!

What's the problem with saying that I am a soul, and nothing more? Do I care if I will get back my body or not? Many people do not even like their bodies. At best, the body is like a shiny new car. It is nice for what it is, for how it serves us, but I am not my car. So, too, my body. I have nothing against the body. I would not mind getting it back. It's a fringe benefit to have a body. But why, according to the Torah, does it seem to be much more than that—so much so that it is the concluding Principle of Faith (the only Principle, by the way, which culminates in the statement that G–d's "memory will be

Life Recycling Life

elevated for ever and ever")? The belief that our bodies will be restored to life is obviously of the utmost importance. And, as we said, each of the Thirteen Principles are special because they have an effect on us twenty-four hours a day in everything we do. What then is this great principle really all about?

The answer is that the entire goal of our physical lives is to be the instruments through which this physical, finite world is converted or transformed—recycled, if you will—into an eternal world. We are the recyclers of the physical world. Thus the Torah calls a human being "a tree of the field." Why specifically a tree? A tree is rooted in the ground and draws nourishment from the ground. It then transforms and transports the nourishment to the branches where it eventually blossoms into beautiful fruits. The tree is a transformer.

So, too, a human being.

"Man is a tree" rooted in this world—he turns physicality into spirituality; he transforms the essential nutrients of the physical realm into spiritual energy which is then transmitted to the highest realms where it takes seed and ultimately blossoms into the stuff of eternity. (And thus, Paradise is called the "Garden" of Eden—eternity is a garden which is nourished by activity originally performed in this finite world.) We are the transformers. It is specifically through our physical life that we draw out the spiritual nourishment and transform it.

Beyond Survival

Matter is neither created nor destroyed; it only changes form. That is a law of physics. It has truth in Torah as well. G–d created matter. Since He created it, none of it will go to waste. It will *all* be transformed, one way or another, into eternity. Thus, not merely will the 180 pound body of a deserving person be resurrected, but every piece of bread, drink of water, etc. which that person consumed will also be resurrected. If he ate a piece of meat from a cow slaughtered properly that cow is transformed into something fit to come back to life in the resurrected world as part of that person's resurrected body's life force. Nothing physical gets lost—as long as it was utilized in the prescribed way.

How do we know what the prescribed way is? Torah. Torah is not a series of ritualistic practices whose goal is to preserve the identity of one ethnic group. Torah is a profound manual instructing us how to convert the energy of physical matter into eternal spirituality. Torah tells you which animals you may eat and how to go about slaughtering them. It tells you what, when, and how to take all the raw material of the world and transform it into fulfillments of G–d's will—for example, how to take mundane wool and turn it into *tzitzis*;[1] how to take a

---

[1] And that explains the teaching that when *Mashiach* comes the non-Jews are going to grab onto the *tzitzis* of a Jew and ask him how they can serve him. A Jew who keeps Torah is at the top of the "meta-ecological" chain. He is a certified recycler, a sure bet to convert the physical into the eternal. When *Mashiach* comes, others will suddenly realize the import of that and grab onto a Jew's *tzitzis*, which are symbolic of all the Torah's *mitzvos*. *Mitzvos* are the technique for transformation, and just as the Jew transforms wool into

house and turn it into a sanctuary; how to take a dinner table and turn it into an alter; how to take time and transform it into *Shabbos;* etc.

That explains why rather than *ascent* of the soul from the body, holiness in the Torah outlook emphasizes *descent* of the soul into the body. The ultimate achievement is to successfully integrate the soul into the body. It is true that sometimes on the road toward that achievement a person may need to de-emphasize and even deny his bodily needs, at least temporarily. However, that is not what G-d wants.[1] The Torah frowns upon asceticism; it commands a person to be involved in every part of life. The first commandment is to "be fruitful and multiply," which means that a person must marry, raise a family, own a home, and have an income. We are husbands, wives, fathers, mothers, laborers, professionals, and business people, as well as spiritual seekers and scholars. And then there are all the holidays—the holy days. *Shabbos,* the holiest of them all, is very physical. It is sanctified Friday night on a cup of wine—strong, intoxicating wine

---

tzitzis—insuring the resurrection of that wool essence in eternity—so, too, the non-Jew will one day recognize that the only guarantee that his physical existence will achieve a measure of eternity is by attaching himself to those who perform *mitzvos.*

[1] And thus a *Nazir*, one who takes a vow to voluntarily abstain from certain bodily pleasures, must conclude his period of abstention by bringing a *sin*-offering. The Torah considers it as if there is an element of sin in his abstention, because G-d created the physical world not to be rejected but to be transformed. Thus even a *Nazir* whose abstention originates from the highest of motivations must bring a sin-offering to impress upon himself that his abstention was a means toward an end, not the end itself.

Beyond Survival

is the ideal. Then we eat, sing, and interact with our family until the following nightfall. It's all very physical. And the more physical, the better. Just as metal, the heaviest of physical substances, is the best conductor of electricity, so, too, is the very bodily nature of our selves the best conductor of spiritual energy.

If we constantly live with the concept of the thirteenth Principle—revival of our physical self—our life here will be an entirely different life because we will realize that everything has its recycling potential. Take money, for instance. We are often so irresponsible with it. We complain that we have no money, but when we get it we spend it recklessly. What is the "sin" there? No penny comes into our hands without some higher purpose intended for it. If it was given to us it must have some ultimate value. And if we use it properly it will not be just another penny; it will have eternal value.

We will have to give an accounting for every second of life we lived, for every breath that we breathed, for every drop of water we drank, every morsel we ate, and every penny which came our way. What did we do with it? How did we utilize it? Everything receives its *tikkun*, its destiny (literally, its repair or restoration), through us. We are the physical world's recyclers.

Armed with this knowledge a person can feel that every second is an accomplishment—even in the most seemingly unproductive situations. For example, usually an incapacitated person in a hospital feels totally worthless. However, that person can be the greatest producer

Life Recycling Life

in this recycling center called life. Picture a little child sick in the hospital and a hundred people are saying extra prayers for him, as well as giving charity, and making promises to G-d, etc. so that the child should recover. The child is a locomotive. He is "pulling" countless others behind him, elevating their otherwise mundane endeavors. He thereby has a share in every action they do, a share in every physical thing they transform—all the doctors, nurses, hospital janitors; even the truck drivers who deliver his food; even those who prepared his food, and those who stocked the food in the supermarket, and those who farmed the food from the ground, etc.—all of their work becomes transformed into life in the eternal world. There is an unseen connection between everything. Each of us is connected to each other in unseen ways. We have no idea what we are elevating through even our simple physical existence.

A woman in deep pain once came to seek counsel from me. She had five children and had recently lost her husband to cancer. Furthermore, one of her children, a three-year-old boy, was in a near vegetable state with a disease which was going to kill him within two years. "Why is G-d punishing me?" she wanted to know.

First, I said, there is no need to view it as a punishment. I explained to her the following: Our Sages teach us that Abraham died five years before his time because his thirteen-year-old grandson, Esau, was beginning to manifest evil behavior in public. G-d spared Abraham knowledge of this evil and shortened his life by five years.

Beyond Survival

Nevertheless, "Abraham came with all his days," the Torah tells us, meaning that he accomplished everything he was created to accomplish without those additional five years. He did not lose a day.

I explained to the woman that although he accomplished all his spiritual goals, he nevertheless was missing five years worth of simply living—of simply breathing oxygen. Mere existence is an accomplishment, a gift from G-d. Despite "coming with all his days," Abraham was missing five years of purely physical existence.

"Now, imagine," I told her, "an auction in heaven for the privilege of living those missing five years of Abraham's life. Even though such a life would entail existing in a vegetable state, Abraham's mere physical life was so holy, so involved in converting physical matter into eternity, that who would not place a bid for the privilege of being associated with his body? Therefore," I said to her, "maybe you have such a child. Do you know how privileged you may be?"

Of course, I did not mean to say she was necessarily taking care specifically of Abraham's body. However, the thought that she was privileged to be entrusted with the bodily existence of some holy soul changed her outlook.

The final Principle of Faith is tied to the first. The first told us that G-d is the Creator and Driving Force of all creation. Nothing happens by coincidence. Nothing is purposeless. The thirteenth Principle is a necessary correlate of a purposeful world. It does not make sense that G-d should have created something to be ultimately

Life Recycling Life

destroyed. Since everything in creation is His it is only logical to assume that it has a destiny in eternity. Every little thing of this physical world has a destiny. It was put here for a purpose. The physical is not an obstacle or a mere temptation; it is not an accident that G‑d created the world in a physical way. The physical is something we *must* have a connection to if we hope to fulfill our purpose in creation.[1]

The thirteenth Principle thus drives home to us how important every part of our life is, especially our physical life. G‑d created us as a body. The reason is so that one day we will transform it (and everything it comes in contact with) into a part of eternity. "All Israel have a portion in eternity," which according to our line of reasoning can be taken to mean: the entirety of our individual lives—*all* [of a single] Israel[ite]—constitutes a literal portion of eternity. When you believe this with conviction, then you will have new respect for yourself—for every aspect of your present life circumstance.

Citizenship

We say every morning in the prayer *Elokai neshama*: "My G‑d, the soul which You have put into me is pure . . ." G‑d put a soul in me. The question is, who is

---

[1] In fact, that amounts to the idea expressed in various philosophical and mystical texts that the purpose of life is to give us the opportunity to become "partners with G‑d in the work of creation." When we convert the matter of the material world into the substance of the Resurrected World we are literally becoming partners with G‑d in the work of creation.

Beyond Survival

the "me"? Who is speaking about the soul in this prayer? I am I. If the soul is something put in "me," who am I? Further on in the same prayer it says, "You will give it [the soul] back *to me* in the time to come." Again, the question is who is the "me"? Who is my soul being returned to? If I am not my soul, who am I?

These questions lead to a truly profound thought. *We are not our souls.* I am not my soul. This human body *possesses* a soul—even identifies with it—but it is not inextricably one with the soul—at least not at first. The soul is put in me; it is that part of G–d within me. But it is not necessarily "me."

If I am not my soul, then for what purpose am I given it to begin with? The answer is: *to acquire it.*

This needs to be understood.

A person who wants to venture into space needs a spaceship. The function of the spaceship is to protect the astronaut by reproducing the environment of his place of origin. The spaceship does this in two ways. First, it isolates the astronaut from the outside, and second, it contains the sustenance necessary for survival. Conversely, imagine a creature who could only survive in space. To survive on earth he would need an "earthship." He needs his sustenance, his original environment plus protection from our environment, built into his "earthship."

There are two worlds: heaven and earth. The two are connected, however—in the human being. A person is made of a body, which eventually dies, and a soul, which is eternal. Our body is the "citizen of earth," while our

Life Recycling Life

soul is the "citizen of space." The human being is a combination of these two "citizens."

The seminal question in life is, to which are you committed—the body or the soul? To which citizenship do you ascribe? And you can only be a citizen of one or the other. Yes, with your protective covering you can venture into both worlds—a physical person can experience spirituality, and a spiritual person can experience physicality—but at the heart where are you at home? And life is a never-ending challenge to not only believe in our hearts that we are citizens of heaven temporarily stationed on earth, but to actualize that feeling in our everyday lives, in every nuance of our everyday lives.

That is the ideal. Of course life continually gets in the way. It challenges us at every turn to identify with the pull of the body. You want to read more books like this (or regularly read this one again and again), but the newspaper is much more convenient and less taxing. You want to save your money to give more to needy causes, but you have an urge to spend it on the things you want. And so on. How is a person expected to win the battle? It seems impossible.

Luckily, one human being, many, many years ago, fought that battle and won it so convincingly that he bequeathed to us the means by which to win our own battle. That person was Abraham.

When G-d created Adam, he drew up straightforward battle lines: "From all the trees in the garden you may eat; but from the Tree of Knowledge you may not eat." In simplistic terms, G–d was telling him: I created you with two contradictory parts. But I want to test you to see which you are committed to? Are you willing to sacrifice the instant gratification of forbidden knowledge, the pull of your body? If you can I will reward you at a later date.

Of course, Adam chose the immediate pleasure of eating the forbidden fruit. By doing so, his eternal soul never really fused into his being. It floated, so to speak, from offspring to offspring until Abraham came along. There were many righteous people who lived between Adam and Abraham, but they never sacrificed their all in order to fuse that eternal soul permanently into their being. Abraham was tested ten times, culminating in the command to sacrifice his one and only beloved son. That immortalized his lifelong effort to prove that he was a genuine citizen of heaven. His reward was that his children would become naturalized "citizens." Thus, that higher soul, which had "floated" from descendant to descendant since Adam, found a permanent resting place in Abraham's being.

Abraham was the first person to successfully declare himself a citizen of heaven. Yes, he was physical. But his primary orientation was spiritual, eternal. And therefore as a citizen of "heaven/space" his descendants had to be given an "earthship." That "earthship" is the Torah of 613 commandments—365 "Thou shalt nots" (which serve as the "earthship's" protective covering) and 248 "Thou shalts," (which serve as the sustenance supplying

Life Recycling Life

the energy needed to survive). These commandments ensure that the Jew orients his or her soul toward spirituality. After all, such a code of laws represents (among other things) submission of personal desire to the Divine will, sacrifice of certain aspects of physicality, etc. That sacrifice, however, is the very thing which declares that he or she is a citizen of heaven, that he or she identifies with his or her eternal soul.

You begin life as a body—a body which *possesses* a soul, but which is not inextricably one with the soul. Nevertheless, that soul can become part of you—one with you—when you live a life which caters to its needs, when you identify yourself as a citizen of its laws. That is never easy. The desires of the body and the desires of the soul are contradictory. What one likes the other does not like, and vice-versa. That is the ongoing conflict each of us feels within. In fact, if we do not feel that conflict something may really be wrong. We may be so numb to our soul's desires that we cease to feel them.

Nevertheless, the real you—your destined self—is your soul. Your body has been lent to you by G-d. It is like a rented car. If you go on vacation for a month and rent a car, do you cry when you have to give the car back at the end of the month? You derived good use from the car while you needed it and then gave it back.

We have taken a trip down to this earth and have rented a vehicle for seventy or eighty years. When the time comes to give it back, we give it back. G-d promises that if we use the body wisely, He will give it back to us in the eternal world. In that world, our physical bodies will be reconstituted in such a way that even they will be spiritual. Then we will be able to talk about them as we talk about our true selves. However, now we are only "renting" them. We should not grow so attached to them that our essential identification is with them.

We are hosts to a part of G–d within us. That is our soul. We have the opportunity to forgo our natural identification with the body in order to identify with the desires of the soul. When we do so, the soul—which was only something "leased" to us at the beginning—becomes ours permanently. It become us; we become it. That is the ultimate reward.

Chapter 9

The Formula For Survival

CHAPTER 9

The Formula For Survival

In the previous chapters we covered the Thirteen Principles of Faith. We endeavored to show that faith, or *emunah*, need not (and should not) be an abstract idea. The question is how does a person know that his *emunah* is more than just an abstract principle? Talk is cheap. When is your belief real and alive?

When you have *bitachon*, explains the Ramban.[1]

Generally, one finds either of two definitions for *bitachon* in the many and varied writings of our Sages recorded over the centuries. And those definitions seem to contradict each other, although both are valid in their own ways.[2] For the purposes of clarity, one I will simply

---
[1] Sefer *Emunah U'bitachon*, Chapter 1.
[2] What I mean is *not* that one set of Sages denies the validity of the others, but that each set chose to emphasize one coloration of the idea over the other. The reason for the different emphases, I believe,

refer to as *bitachon*,¹ or "reliance," and the other I will refer to as *chisayon*,² which means "shelter," as used in the verse, "It is better to be sheltered (*lachsos*—i.e. *chisayon*) by G–d than to trust in man or princes."

Bitachon And Chisayon

Simple *bitachon* means that a person believes that G–d listens to him or her. Such people cast all their burdens upon G–d. They cry out, beg, nag, and perhaps even demand in the confident expectation that G–d will answer their request. It is not much different than a young child's relationship with his parent. And G–d is oftentimes willing to bend to such a person's request, not necessarily because of the person's merit, but to show that He is involved with every individual.

The Vilna Gaon writes that some of the best prayers are offered by thieves. Imagine a thief in the middle of a robbery when all of a sudden he hears footsteps. "G–d, please help me!" he prays. That is the most powerful prayer because "G–d is close to all those who call out to

---

was due to the different circumstances and variant living conditions of the people in their time and place. They were like doctors who possess the expertise to know exactly which medicine to prescribe for which patient at which time.

[1] The following authorities subscribe to this definition: Rabbenu Yonah, R. Yosef Albo (*Sefer HaIkkarim*), Rabbenu Bachya, the Alshech HaKodesh, R. Chaim Vital, R. Yisroel Salanter, and the Alter of Navarodok.

[2] The following authorities subscribe to this definition: Rashi (see following), the Chovos HaLevavos, the Maharal, the Vilna Gaon, and the Chazon Ish.

The Formula For Survival

Him, to all who call out to Him *in truth*." And there is no one who is more desperately calling out in truth than the thief at that moment. Absolute desperation breeds the best prayers, and those types of prayers are the ones which are usually answered fastest.

There is a dynamic in turning to G–d. When people get their prayers answered—even prayers for insignificant or hypocritical[1] things—they sense G–d's presence much more so than before. Having come to a greater awareness of G–d's presence, they are more likely to turn to Him repeatedly in the future. The end result is that through an almost childlike reliance upon G–d in the expectation that one's requests will be answered, the purpose of creation—awareness of G–d—is advanced. That is *bitachon*.

Chisayon, on the other hand, means that a person recognizes he is under G–d's protective wings. Such a person is tranquil and unworried even in the worst situations. A person with *chisayon* knows that G–d controls everything and brings about events only for his ultimate good. Do we know what is best for us? Do we really know where our life is leading? The one thing we do know is that nothing happens to us without G–d's presence or awareness. And therefore we accept whatever happens. That attitude produces an unshakable tranquillity.

---

[1] "One who puts his trust in G–d is surrounded by kindness (i.e. is extended kindness—*chesed*—by G–d). Even a wrongdoer (*rasha*) who trusts in G–d is surrounded by kindness." (*Yalkut Shimoni, Tehillim* 719)

Beyond Survival

Picture a person about to lose his house to foreclosure unless he comes up with $100,000 by morning. It is the night before foreclosure and he has no money. Can such a person sleep tranquilly? Yes. And there are three types of "tranquilizers" he can take to help him sleep.

One is to contact a very wealthy person in the community known for his big heart, tell him your troubles, and be told in reply, "Don't worry. I will not let them take away your house. Come tomorrow, first thing in the morning, I will personally write out a $100,000 bank note you can use to save your house."

The second way to feel secure enough to fall asleep that night is to visit a *tzaddik*—a genuine, holy person, whose prayers are listened to—pour out your heart to him, and hear him say, "Don't worry. I promise that you will not be thrown out of your house. Go home and sleep well. You have my blessing."

Of these two choices, which is preferable? Whenever I ask that question to an audience I get a fairly consistent response. The men opt for the first "tranquilizer," and the women for the second. Men want the money, and women want the *tzaddik*.

In any event, there is a third type of reassurance. It is the person with the trust in G–d classified as *chisayon*. That person knows that if he tried every possible channel to come up with the money and nothing worked he is prepared to accept whatever happens. There is no fighting G–d. If G–d wants him out of the house, he does not mind. And if G–d does not want him out of the house

The Formula For Survival

something will happen to prevent the bank from foreclosing.

Let me make myself perfectly clear. *Chisayon* does *not* mean that such a person does *not* ask the wealthy man for money or the *tzaddik* for a blessing. Rather he does try to contact the wealthy man and to visit the *tzaddik*. And he may even get the promise of money and the blessing. Even so, it is the awareness that he is under G–d's protective wings which helps him sleep peacefully that night. Nothing is guaranteed. Perhaps, come morning, the wealthy man will renege or for some reason the *tzaddik's* blessing will not be fulfilled by G–d. But when a person knows that his destiny is completely in the hand of G–d, there is nothing more reassuring.

And that is essentially how the Vilna Gaon explains the verse, "It is better to be sheltered (i.e. *chisayon*) by G–d than to trust in man or princes." *Chisayon* is the best medicine. It is better than "trusting in man," i.e. the wealthy man who promises you a check in the morning, and it is even better than the blessing of the "princes" (i.e. the *tzaddik*). *Chisayon* is the self-assured confidence that G–d is directly involved in everything which happens to a person and arranges everything in his ultimate best interests.

The question is, how does a person with *chisayon* understand his basic human needs? After all, is a person who is about to lose his house supposed to deny the fact that he needs the house? How, then, is a person with *chisayon* expected to pray to G–d if he truly believes that G–d takes care of his needs anyway?

The answer is that such a person tells himself, "Who am I to dictate to G–d what is best? Nevertheless, I must pray for my needs as I feel them, because I have a separate commandment to pray.[1] However, in all my prayers is the self-understood qualification that if my needs conflict with what G–d feels is in my best interest, then I forgo my requests. I have no demands, only an obligation to seek to have my needs satisfied." In other words, using our example, the man must seek out the wealthy patron and the *tzaddik* to save his house; and above all he must pray to G–d for some miracle to prevent foreclosure. That is his obligation, for it is a basic human need he is asking for. However, he is prepared to accept any outcome. He asks, but does not demand. If after all these efforts he loses his house, he is confident that G–d has allowed it to happen for his ultimate good. And that knowledge reassures him more than anything.

And such an attitude makes sense. Who would advise a parent to acquiesce to all his children's demands? If a child screams and yells that he wants ice cream before breakfast, does a judicious parent give in to the demand? So, too, with G–d. When we examine our personal history, most of us will admit that the things we complained about the most turned out to be the very things which came to mean the most—the biggest disappointment blossomed into the greatest achievement. G–d wants us

---

[1] See Chapter 4, *Prayer*.

The Formula For Survival

to come forward and express our needs to Him, but that does not mean He has to give them to us. When a beloved one is sick, we are expected—and are indeed obligated—to ask G–d to heal the person. However, if he wasn't healed, and the beloved one even passed away, G–d forbid, does that mean our prayer was wasted or a failure? Absolutely not. We accept what G–d does, because only He knows what is in a person's ultimate best interest. That is *chisayon*.

Bitachon entails *making* demands of G–d. *Chisayon* entails *accepting* G–d's demands on us.[1] Both prove that

---

[1] The difference between *bitachon* and *chisayon* is poignantly illustrated in the following Talmudic passage:
"There is no Power except G–d." Rabbi Chanina added, "Even sorcery." There was a sorceress who tried to obtain dirt from underneath the bed of Rabbi Chanina [in order to use it in a spell intended to harm him]. He [caught her in the act and] said to her, "Take! You cannot harm me." Rabbi Yochanan [found that story problematic. He] said, Why is sorcery called sorcery (*kishafim*)? Because it can "oppose" (*makchishim*, related to *kishafim*) the Powers Above. [Thus, Rabbi Chanina should not have been so confident. However, the resolution to the problem is that] Rabbi Chanina was an exception. He had much merit [so much, that he was protected from the powers of sorcery]. (*Chullin* 7b)

The sorceress needed the dirt to perform witchcraft on Rabbi Chanina. When Rabbi Chanina caught her the natural reaction would have been to stop her. After all, the dirt is like a gun. She is going to use it to harm him. It would only be natural for Rabbi Chanina to try to take away the dirt like we would try to disarm a robber. But he didn't do that. He said, "Take! Take all the dirt you want. You cannot harm me." Which type of faith does that reflect—*bitachon* or *chisayon*? *Bitachon*. Rabbi Chanina told her to take the earth because she could not harm him. It was as if he was saying to her, "Take the gun. Try to shoot. I am sure G–d will not let it fire.

Beyond Survival

you possess more than just an abstract philosophical faith in G‑d because (whether you pray to G‑d with the child's expectation of getting an answer or you remain calm in a difficult situation on the strength of your G‑d-awareness) you are applying your intellectual understanding of belief.

The truth is that *bitachon* and *chisayon* go hand-in-hand. The end goal of life is to obtain the greatest possible awareness of G‑d's presence. G‑d wants to introduce Himself to us. He wants us to be convinced that He is listening. The first step, then, is for Him to do what we want. He answers our prayers in a miraculous fashion. And I do not believe that there is a single individual who cannot tell certain stories in his life which clearly demonstrated that G‑d was listening to him. Here and there miracles happen to everyone. A person asked, begged, etc.—and, lo and behold, his prayers were answered. G‑d listened. Admittedly, sometimes such miracles are not always noticeable until later, and can only be seen in retrospect. But they were miracles nonetheless.

You cannot harm me."

Interestingly, the exact story is recounted in another place, *Sanhedrin* (67b), with one small but very significant difference. In the first account, after Rabbi Chanina caught the sorceress stealing the dirt he said to her, "Take! You cannot hurt me." In this second account (*Sanhedrin*), he says, "Take! *If you can hurt me, go do it.*" The slight change in wording of the second account reflects *chisayon*. And Rashi spells it out for us clearly: "If you will be successful with your sorcery," Rashi explains Rabbi Chanina's words, "do it because no one can do anything except G‑d. If G‑d wants to protect me, you cannot hurt me. And if you do hurt me it is only G‑d who does it, not you. And if G‑d does it, I accept it."

The Formula For Survival

However, after G-d has proven to us that He is attuned to our prayers, *the next step is for us to prove to Him that we are attuned to Him*. It is a two-way relationship. The first level, *bitachon*, is lower than *chisayon*. Why? Because *bitachon* proves G-d, not the person. A miracle proves G-d intervenes. But it does not necessarily prove that the person was worthy. A person's faith is vindicated only when he continues to rely on G-d even when *He does not immediately or seemingly answer our prayers*. Our job is to show the world that we live with G-d. Oftentimes, the greatest way to prove that is to show others that we are not devastated because of what we lack.

Simple *bitachon* is very important. We turn to G-d, make strong requests or demands, and are answered. G-d introduces Himself to us. But once He introduces Himself—once we know that G-d is listening—then we have to believe in Him even when we do not see Him (i.e. even when our wishes and prayers do not receive immediate or apparent fulfillment). That is *chisayon*. *Chisayon* is the acid test of faith because when a person's face radiates confidence and tranquillity even when he does not get what he wants, or does not understand why G-d does something, it is an accomplishment worth writing home about.

Nevertheless, simple *bitachon*—turning to G-d out of a feeling of need or desperation—is very important. It is generally the first part of a two step process. First, we get convinced that G-d listens to us.[1] That is *bitachon*.

---

[1] This is why our nationhood began amidst the miracles of the exo-

Beyond Survival

Second, we have to prove that we listen to G–d.[1] That is *chisayon*.[2]

Bitachon In The End Of Days

The Vilna Gaon writes:

"The underlying reason the Torah commandments (*mitzvos*) were given to the Jewish People is so that they should become wholehearted believers (*bitchonim*) in G–d ... [and] so that the final generation should know that the purpose of everything is to produce The Complete Trust (*habitachon hashalem*). And that is the essence of all the *mitzvos*."[3]

---

dus, the giving of the Torah, and the forty years in the desert.

[1] That is why we eventually went into the exile which we have been in now for almost 2,000 years. See *Darkness Before Dawn* for the fuller explanation of this.

[2] Generally, *chisayon*, as we said, is a more developed level of faith. However, according to the Chazon Ish, there are people who are on the level to make demands of G–d, so to speak. But they are very, very few. Who are they? What are the qualifications? I would say that they are those who know not to ask what G–d does not want to do. In other words, their greatness is that they know what G–d wants.

That can explain why we hear a great person who performs some miraculous intervention for one person, but not for another even thought he may be in seemingly the exact same desperate position as the first person. The *tzaddik* did not discriminate. It's just that he knows he cannot dictate to G–d what to do. He happens to know or intuit what G–d's plan is for the person seeking his help, so he adds his personal blessing. He did not make demands, though. He simply knew that G–d wanted more *chisayon* out of the person he did not give the blessing to.

[3] Commentary to Proverbs 22:19.

The Formula For Survival

G–d did not create the world for the animals. Humanity is the purpose of creation. But humanity has a purpose and function too—it has to produce something for its Creator. That "something" is to become *bitchonim*, wholehearted believers.

By definition, G–d needs nothing. However, He intentionally created the world with a deficiency that only His creations could fill—and that is, to coronate Him king.[1] However, there is no king without subjects. If those in his domain reject his kingship he cannot give to them. G–d's kingship depends upon the free will of humanity. And thus as ready and willing as He is to be our king, *He is dependent upon us* to coronate Him king. We are the ones who bring G–d into our lives, or we are the ones who deny Him access to our lives.

Bitachon (whether in the simple sense or in the sense of *chisayon*) boils down to a sensation encompassing the most palpable human emotion acknowledging G–d's existence. And that is really what it means to coronate Him king. The more a person feels G–d's existence, the greater the desire of that person to coronate Him king. And that explains the strong statement of the Vilna Gaon, quoted above. The entire purpose of Torah,

---

[1] A king is not a tyrant. A truly, benevolent king ultimately gives more to his subjects than they give to him. The idea of G–d as King holds the greatest possible promise for world peace. In fact, it is ultimately the only hope for humanity's redemption. Yet, until humanity willingly accepts His kingship, He cannot give to humanity as He desires. And He does desire to give, more so than we ourselves so desire. (See the supplemental essay on Rosh HaShannah in *Choose Life!* for a more detailed explanation of what it means to coronate G–d.)

Beyond Survival

mitzvos, and in fact everything is to become *bitchonim*, wholehearted believers who acknowledge their total dependence on G–d. *Bitachon* is another way of saying that a person coronates G–d as king in his or her life. When we live our lives as if reacting to the presence of the Unseen G–d we not only justify our existence, but actually give G–d something He cannot procure for Himself. We acknowledge His kingship.

Ironically, never before in history has it been easier to deny G–d and His kingship. With all our advances in technology, medicine, computers, space travel, communications, etc. no generation has ever had so much knowledge and power, to the point that it appears to be independent of G–d. No civilization has had the opportunity to be so arrogant, to become so intoxicated with its successes.

By contrast, no generation was as privy to open miracles as the Generation in the Desert. For forty years they were fed manna from heaven, surrounded by clouds of glory, never had their clothes or shoes wear out, etc. G–d performed all the miracles. He showed that He ran the system; that He was the "Driving Force" of everything.

Today, science and technology would have us believe that it can all be run without G–d. And the reason that G–d allows sciences and inventions to possess the aura of divinity is because history as we know it is winding down toward its conclusion. Yes, never before has it been easier to deny G–d. But, likewise, never before has there been such an opportunity to acknowledge that G–d runs the

The Formula For Survival

system even when the system—superficially at least—appears to run on its own.

That is why the Vilna Gaon writes "... so that the latter generation (*dor acharon*) should know that the entire purpose of everything is to produce The Complete Belief (*habitachon hashalem*)." In order to produce that absolutely unblemished *bitachon* we are tested in the very things which get to the root of our existence. Our generation's challenges are unique. We are the ones given the final exam. And that is why science, technology, and in fact every nuance of life today challenges our *bitachon*. It is a test of the greatest proportions, which no other generation has had.

There is no way to minimize the challenge—the battle—before us. Half the battle is won, though, when we identify the strategy of our enemy. The enemy wants to undermine our *bitachon*. That is his entire goal. It is the target against which he has arrayed all his forces. And that is why securing our *bitachon* is a matter of the highest priority. In fact, our very survival depends on it. We must purify our hearts to believe and trust in G–d no matter what happens.

In a fascinating way, Rashi teaches that to us. Usually Rashi's commentary is geared to supplying the simplest understanding of a given verse. However, he often deviates from that pattern whenever he describes an event having to do with the End of Days.[1] In fact, he will not

---

[1] See, for instance, Rashi on Malachi 3:22-24, and our related discussion in *Days Are Coming* (Part I, Chapter 2, subchapter, "Malachi:

only stray from the simple explanation but will even offer the most extreme interpretation.

One such example is his commentary on the verse: *Tamim t'hiyeh im Hashem Elokecha*, "Be wholehearted with your G-d."[1] The verse is both an order and a promise. Though not technically one of the 613 commandments, the verse exhorts us to "be wholehearted" at the same time it promises us that eventually, at the End of Days, we "will be wholehearted with G-d."[2]

Now, Rashi explains *taamim t'hiyeh* to mean "going wholeheartedly with G-d, only looking to Him, not worrying or even wanting to know what the future will bring, because no matter what happens to you you accept it." That is the ultimate state of being: to not worry about the future because you trust—have *bitachon*[3]—that every happening is part of G-d's plan for you.

When you are able to stop worrying about the future you can begin to live in the present, to appreciate the moment before you. That is called choosing life, i.e.

The Hearts of the Fathers.")
[1] Deut. 18:13.
[2] Similarly, two other famous exhortations—"choose life!" and "Be holy!"—are technically not part of the 613 commandments either. They too promise us that eventually, at the End of Days, we will indeed "choose life" and "be holy." The fact that these three are not in the 613 indicates their elevated status, however. They are all-inclusive. They are not merely commandments, but states of being which we will attain at the End of Days. Until we reach the End of Days, though, we have to work on earning those states of being. We have to be wholehearted, choose life, and be holy as much as we can until G-d makes it natural for us some day.
[3] Actually, *chisayon*, in the sense used above, would be more precise.

The Formula For Survival

choosing the life of the present rather than choosing to worry over the future, a future which G–d can totally manipulate anyway.

According to Rashi, belief does not mean that we trust that G–d will give us what we want. It means we accept that everything which happens—whether for our immediate good or immediate bad—is done by G–d based on a calculation of our *ultimate* good. *Bitachon* is our ability to recognize that there is no such thing as coincidence. G–d is the only reality. We must therefore ascribe all our success to G–d, while at the same time being ever ready to accept that our disappointments too are orchestrated by Him as part of His overall plan for the greatest good.

Of course, we are human beings. We have feelings. It would be inhuman to deny feeling the pain of a tragedy or the distress over some adverse circumstance. However, our choice is how long we remain pained. Do we prolong it and linger incapacitated, drowning ourselves in sorrow and sabotaging our well-being so that others will feel sorry for us? Or do we release it relatively quickly and go on with our lives? The more true *bitachon* you have, the more quickly you will be able to release the pain.

Bitachon is like exercise. It requires daily repetition. Think about it. Meditate on it. Listen to a tape about it. Read a book about it. And do not worry about reading the same book, listening to the same tape, or thinking about the same phrase over and over again. We need continuous exercise. Never let yourself get tired of it. Always reach for the new depth of understanding. Life's challenges are never-ending, and when we listen to the same tape[1] we heard last month it has new meaning for us. You can satiate yourself every time. Just make sure to do your daily *bitachon* exercises and get your spiritual nourishment. It is medicine for the soul. Your life depends on it.[2]

---

[1] The original series of tapes from which this book came to be written is available for sale. See ordering information at the end of this book.

[2] This book has been specially designed to make regular review of its ideas accessible and enjoyable. Thus, as you surely have noticed, the running text is supplemented with footnotes, many of which significantly deepen the ideas touched on in the main body. Consequently, if the reader wants to review the entire book (or a particular chapter) relatively quickly, the footnotes can be skipped. Conversely, if the reader reads the book through the first time without bothering too much with the footnotes, a second reading which includes study of the footnotes will probably yield a deeper, more satisfying understanding. Take advantage of this format. The bottom line is that whether you make this book or another a favored text, make sure you have a favored text which refreshes your *emunah* and *bitachon*.

Shalheves Information And Catalogue

Shalheves:
Enhancing Lives Through Meaning and Torah[1]

Jonathon Pollard, languishing in solitary confinement, once received a book from a friend. Before finishing it, he wrote back to her: "I can't even begin to tell you how deeply touched I was by your gift of Rabbi Tauber's *Choose Life!* I've already read about half the book and find it to be thoroughly delightful. I know this probably won't surprise you, but Rabbi Tauber's message has managed to give me a much needed psychological boost—and that's saying a lot, believe me!"

Rabbi Ezriel Tauber has always exhibited a knack for giving hope and meaning to the downtrodden and estranged. As a holocaust survivor he knows the meaning of desperation. As a businessman he has a unique sensitivity to the everyday person in the street. Finally, as a penetrating thinker thoroughly familiar with the gamut of Jewish philosophy from *Chovos HeLevavos* to the Maharal and Ramchal, he has a way of expressing the deep and beautiful Torah philosophy of life in an eminently practical and inspiring manner.

The core of his outlook can be found in the six books he has authored to date. "These books speak to everyone," he says. "They are geared for *frum* people, but I have found the material effective with all types. Recently, I conducted a

---

[1] The following article, by Yaakov Astor, originally appeared in *Good Fortune Magazine*, November 1993.

workshop in Miami with best-selling author Dr. Brian L. Weiss, whose book *Many Lives, Many Masters* has convinced hundreds of thousands of people worldwide that there is life after death. All I did was tell over the Torah viewpoint and it was an immense success. While it is true that on one hand the world is deteriorating in many respects, on the other hand thinking people from all fields are making discoveries which confirm Torah. The material in my books takes advantage of this societal upheaval and gives people real meaning in life."

Much of the material in the books originally grew out of lectures (delivered by Rabbi Tauber under the auspices of his organization, Shalheves) targeted to specific groups in need: the lost, the alone, the bereaved, the divorced, the childless, the family in crisis, etc. Into this fertile soil of human anguish he planted seeds which have not only blossomed themselves but have seeded others elsewhere. Several individuals now have themselves become lecturers and leaders of self-help and support groups. Each has found in the thoughts of Rabbi Tauber a starting point of renewal.

Renewal is his message, yet according to Rabbi Tauber there is nothing new in his outlook. "We never needed psychologists in the past," he remarks. "Torah was our psychology. And whoever learned it was able to become their own psychologist. That is one of my goals. To help people become their own Torah psychologists."

Sounds nice. But can you really expect everyone to become their own psychologist? To Rabbi Tauber the answer is, "Yes."

The secret, he believes, is not so secret. It is merely developing the *clarity* that every event is meaningful. Everyone experiences misfortune. It is generally not in our hands to avoid the major setbacks in life. "All is in the hands of heaven except fear of heaven." What is in our hands, though, is the ability to know that hardship is G–d's way of allowing us to come to our own understanding of a lesson we need to learn.

Enhancing Lives

"The problem is that people first go outside of Torah," Rabbi Tauber explains, "in search of the psychology or philosophy that will help them feel better about their problems. I have nothing against self-help techniques and mind healing 'technologies' as part of an overall program toward mental health. But when the goal is to make people happy you create nothing but a laughing hyena. On the other hand, give people some real meaning and they can find happiness even without all those psychologies and techniques. The goal is *not* to make people happy, but to make people complete, which automatically leads to happiness."

Rabbi Tauber does concede that he finds the writings of one psychologist to be very close to the Torah ideal: Viktor Frankl, author of *Man's Search For Meaning*, and innovator of the school of psychology known as Logotherapy. To Dr. Frankl the need for meaning is the primary drive in a person. However, whereas to Frankl meaning is personal truth—it is exclusively the "Unconscious God" (to use a title of one of his books) residing within—to Judaism truth is "Objective G-d" and can be found in the Torah. A person who fashions his own ideals, like a fashioner of idols, is making G-d into his image rather than making himself into G-d's image. Despite that, Rabbi Tauber finds value in Frankl's basic view that the human being is first and foremost a being—whether conscious or unconscious of the fact—in search of meaning.

If lack of meaning is the hole in each person's life, then, to use one of Rabbi Tauber's favorite *mosholim*, Torah is the puzzle piece which interlocks perfectly into that empty slot. According to Rabbi Tauber, "Everyone's life has been specially arranged since the time of creation so that billions of moments, each with its unique response, have been laid out for him. Yet, it is up to the person to discover the value of every moment." How does one discover that value, especially in times of personal hardship? Through thorough familiarity with the Torah outlook, through thinking like the Torah.

Seeing life through the lens of Torah is an ongoing process and in truth there are no shortcuts. However, Rabbi Tauber views his books as a great way for anyone, be they a beginner or budding scholar, to jump start the process. In his estimation they give one the tools to be one's own Torah psychologist for virtually any situation which arises, because they teach one how to find meaning in every situation. A quick summary of his books illustrates this point.

The first book, *I Shall Not Want*, addresses the Torah outlook on working for a living. The working world can be a boon or a bust. Theological abstractions and esoteric principles of holiness do not easily translate into the challenges commonly found in the modern day workplace. In a straightforward, readable fashion, Rabbi Tauber shows how work can be converted into a spiritual as well as physical blessing.

In *To Become One*, many modern day misconceptions related to the issues of intimacy and marriage are tackled. For instance, abstinence is not the Torah ideal. Marriage was created not as a concession to human passion, but as the perfect complement to it. How much more beautiful life is when the meaning behind the pleasures and pains of the marital bond become clear.

Choose Life! sets down the foundation for Rabbi Tauber's belief that the essence of happiness is the discovery of meaning. This book has changed lives literally overnight. Jonathan Pollard, mentioned above, is one example. A 30 year-old man with a serious illness and resigned to his fate suddenly deciding to fight for his life after reading the book is another example. The most crestfallen and estranged people of all backgrounds have found this book to speak to their heart.

Days Are Coming examines the meaning of the great and rapid societal upheavals taking place in our day. Rather than isolated happenings in a chaotic world, today's headlines begin to make sense when seen against the backdrop of the large brushstrokes of history.

Enhancing Lives

Darkness Before Dawn is Rabbi Tauber's personal view of the holocaust. Again, showing how it is part of a larger historical process he sheds light on the meaning of the world's greatest slaughter. Going beyond that, though, he shows how the lessons of the holocaust can be applied for all grieving and destitute people.

The theme of *Self-Esteem* is plainly suggested by the title. However, more than a manual of ideas on feeling good about oneself, the lessons are taught through the medium of four different adults (based on true case histories) whose difficulties in life have negated their feelings of self-worth, making them anxious and unhappy. In this book, as with all the others, the common theme is: Every situation is pregnant with ultimate meaning. Discover that meaning, or at least have true faith that it is there, and you can weather any storm. You can be a free person.

The truly free person is the person who sees the actual spiritual message behind the veil of circumstance and misfortune; who sees the hand of G–d pulling the strings. He or she radiates a confidence to which others are attracted. Perhaps that explains why Rabbi Tauber's lectures have spawned others to write their own books, lead their own support groups, give their own lectures, and become their own self-made psychologists and counselors.

"Wherever I have spoken, and to whomever I have given my books," he says, "the reaction is very positive. This information needs to be widely publicized. I do not consider it a luxury. It is essential for one's well being in these physically and spiritually difficult times. Every person is obligated to take time out to study his purpose in life. It is the only way to obtain tranquillity."

If nothing else, Rabbi Tauber's work is a breeding ground of personal growth. That alone is a calming insight in these turbulent times.

Beyond Survival

available on tape

Beyond Survival was based on a series of lectures on the Thirteen Principles delivered by Rabbi Ezriel Tauber. That eight tape series is now available on audio cassette for one special price: $27.50 (plus $2.50 for shipping and handling). Listening to the tapes is the ideal way to easily and effectively review the inspiring thoughts you read in the book. Moreover, the tape set comes complete in its own album, and can be personalized to be sent as a gift to a friend or relative you care about (just tell us who to indicate as the sender, the receiver, and the pertinent mailing information, etc.). Whether for yourself (when driving in the car or working at home) and/or for a friend, the tape series is sure to be a gift of lasting value.

AUDIO TAPES
BY RABBI EZRIEL TAUBER

The following is a partial listing of tapes in English by Rabbi Ezriel Tauber, including lectures through the Winter of 5754 (1994). Also available are tapes in Hebrew, Yiddish, and Russian, as well as videos (see end of list). Prices are $4.00 per tape and $15.00 per video (plus shipping and handling). Visa and Mastercard accepted. For further information contact:

Shalheves
P.O. Box 361
Monsey, NY 10952
Phone: (914) 356-3515
Fax: (914) 425-2094

FOR BEGINNERS

75	Introductory Lecture To Non-Committed Jews	796	Be A Proud Jew
		817-A	Torah Concept Of Marriage
		817-B	Reliance On Effort
93	Business And Torah	818	The Value Of Life
146	For Beginners	855	Lets Represent G–D
165-A	The Creation And Its Purpose	872-A	Know G–D
165-B	The Creation And Its Purpose	872-B	Our Crucial Days
167	Business And Torah	966-A	Codes In The Torah
170	Life After Death	966-B	Codes In The Torah
176	Is There Everyday Life?	1003	The Meaning Of Happiness
201	Purpose Of Life (Part 1)	1101	Destiny Of Life
202	Mysticism In Everyday Life (Part 2)	1316	Appreciate Life
		1341-A	Codes In The Torah
203	Mysticism In Everyday Life (Part 3)	1341-B	Codes In The Torah
		1431	You Can Be A Prophet
241	Who Am I?	1452	Two Parts Of Life
250	New Times Of Teshuva	1455	Are We Chosen?
269	Should We Isolate Or Integrate?	1461	We, In Making Moshiach
		1467	Only One Goal In Life
295	Real Life	1489	To Live For Now
307	Jewish Concept Of Woman	1497	We—As Hashem's Ambassadors
316	The Structure Of The Jewish Nation	1502	A Life Which Is All Good
		1506	Why Yaakov Tricks Eisav
317	To Appreciate Our Role	1508	Yaakov Vs. Eisov
323	Should We Plan?	1511	The Real Reason For Anti-Semitism
338	The Value Of Time		
354-A	Codes Revealed In The Torah	1522	Questions And Answers
354-B	Codes Revealed In The Torah	1532	Torah As A Map
394	The Definition Of "Yehudi"	1549	Mishpotim
757-A	Creation And Its Purpose	1581	Avrohom—Today
757-B	Creation And Its Purpose	1603	The Spies Of Today
758-A	Definition Of A Jewish Nation	1668	The Foundation Of Life
758-B	The Benefit Of Suffering	1671	Could A Holocaust Happen Without G–D?
759-A	Torah Concept Of Marriage		
759-B	Torah Concept Of Marriage		

AUDIO TAPES BY RABBI EZRIEL TAUBER

INTERMEDIATE AND ADVANCED

EMUNAH & BITACHON

26	Thirteen Principles Of Faith
241	Who Am I?
782	Believing In Hashem
799	The Full Emunah
832	The First Principal Of Belief
1223	Believing
1292	Bitachon In Stressful Situations
1368	Applying Bitachon To Our Daily Struggles
1434	First Aid For Worriers
1445	Real Bitachon
1457	Finding Hashem When We Feel Alone
1541	The Need Of Bitachon Today
1565	Bitachon Is The Answer
1587	Money Covers Everything
1594	How To Practice Bitachon (Advanced)
1625	Belief In The Darkness
1645	The Definition Of Belief (8 tapes on The 13 Principles Of Faith; ask for album info.)
1654	Survival Today
1685	The Reality Of G–D
1686	Mitzvas Yichud Hashem
1693	How To Develop Faith
1695	Suffering Develops Faith
1696	Emunah In Practical Life
1700	Knowledge & Faith (included in the 8 tapes of The 13 Principles album; see 1645)

THE PURPOSE OF CREATION

144	The Tree Which Is A Fruit
518	The Purpose Of Creation
519	Yisroel—Fulfillment Of Creation
607	Life In Gan Eden
757-A	Creation And Its Purpose
757-B	Creation And Its Purpose
821-A	The Meaning Of Life
821-B	The Meaning Of Life
904-A	Creation And Its Purpose
904-B	Creation And Its Purpose
1098	Creation And Its Purpose
1338	A Time For Renewal
1438	Us In Creation
1586-A	The Jew And The World
1586-B	The Jew And The World
1722	The Process Of Creation

THE JEWISH NATION

269	Should We Isolate Or Integrate
648	The Jewish Nation's Responsibility To The World
758-A	Definition Of A Jewish Nation
758-B	The Benefit Of Suffering
805	My Share In The World To Come
872-A	Know G–D
872-B	Our Crucial Days
900	Let's Build Am Yisroel
901	Be Aware Of Your Duties
959	Leaving Egypt Today
1673	Live A Whole Life
1726	The Meaning Of Being Chosen

THE VALUE OF LIFE

903	Definition Of Truth And The Essence Of Life
997	Every Inch Of Life—Ongoing Bliss To Avodas Hashem
1000	The Value Of A Moment
1008	Every Moment A Mission To Hashem
1029	Is There Freedom Of Choice
1073	Positive Speech
1154	Value Of A Moment Of Life
1218	How To Grow Every Minute
1242	The Ultimate Goal
1243	The Real Free Choice
1315	Appreciate Life
1330	The Meaning Of Life
1340	Find Meaning In Life
1376	The Value Of Life
1682	The Value Of Life
1704	The Value Of Life

THE MEANING OF A JEW

640	Live With Confidence
690	Effort Of Competition

AUDIO TAPES
BY RABBI EZRIEL TAUBER

1380	Meaning Of A Jew
1578	My Greatness
1579	I—The Original Jew

THE GREATNESS OF MAN

670	All Israel Has A Share In The World To Come
737	Love Your Friend As Yourself
753	Discover Yourself
902	How Hashem Tells Me What To Do
913	Ner Hashem Nishmas Adam
945	The Meaning Of The Image Of Hashem
1280	I, As The Only Man On The Planet
1322	You Come First
1333	The Greatness Of Man

HAPPINESS

544	A Happy Life
552	Enrich Your Life
691	Stay High—Always
789	The Real Simcha
820	Plant Life
836	A Moment Of Life
951	Appreciate Your Role
1002	The Meaning Of Happiness
1018	Search For Happiness
1093	Finding Strength
1119	Finding Strength
1725	How To Obtain Happiness From Life

THE BENEFIT OF SUFFERING

554	Suffering As Currency
688	Thank Hashem For Everything
909-A	Sufferings And Tests During The Times Of Moshiach
909-B	Sufferings And Tests During The Times Of Moshiach
952	Suffering As A Currency
995	Carrying Diamonds
1100-A	Golus, Benefit Of Suffering
1100-B	Golus, Benefit Of Suffering
1107	How To Accept A Loss In The Family
1129	Our Life As A Plant
1169	You As An Artist
1300	The Benefit Of Suffering
1328	"Golus," The Benefit Of Suffering
1413	Chizuk In Stressful Situations
1441	The Benefit Of Suffering
1547	How To Accept Our Challenging Days

AHAVAS YISROEL

943	Veahavta Lereacha Komocha
988	Ahavas Yisroel
1077	Chessed To Yourself
1120	Sensitivity To People's Needs
1230	How To Love A Jew
1298	Being Thankful
1658	To Love Your Fellow Jew

WAITING FOR MOSHIACH

243	Our Share In Moshiach
822	Crucial Times Of Today
823	Our Days Of Moshiach
1070	Days Of Moshiach
1082	How To Prepare For Our Times
1128	Our Crucial Days
1133	How To Wait For Moshiach
1136	Our Times In Depth
1142	Times For Action
1149	What Are We Really Waiting For
1153	Waiting For Moshiach
1157	My Share In Moshiach
1437	Are We Ready For Moshiach?
1656	Our Crucial Days

PARNASSA

232	Bitochon Vs. Effort
523	Effort And Bitochon
558	The Manna Of Today
906	Effort And Bitochon Towards Parnassa
953-A	Reliance And Effort
953-B	Reliance And Effort
1106	Finding Hashem In Business
1246	The Man In Nature
1274	Torah In Business
1439	Tranquility In Business

AUDIO TAPES
BY RABBI EZRIEL TAUBER

TESHUVA

188	Our Responsibility Towards The World
250	New Time Of Teshuva
258-A	The Teshuva Prophecy Realized
258-B	The Teshuva Prophecy Realized

TEFILLAH

772	An Effective Prayer
1102	Depth Of Tefillah
1551	The Power Of Tefillah
1558	How To Pray
1595	How Prayer Works (Part 1) (Advanced)
1596	How Prayer Works (Part 2) (Advanced)

LASHON HORAH

837	I, As A Messenger
1240	Why Loshon Horah?

CHINUCH

101	A Lecture To Teachers Of Girls
740	"Chinuch"—The Real Way
960	When Children Question Our Values
1006-A	Chinuch—The Courage To Say No
1006-B	Chinuch—The Courage To Say No
1014	Chinuch For Yourself
1030	The Right Chinuch
1031	Chinuch And Tznius
1590	Parents As Role Models
1599	The Method Of Education
1698	The Parents' Role In Finding The Right Shidduch
1707	The Challenge Of Raising Young Adults
1717	The Final Solution Or Resolution?

MARRIAGE

759-A	Torah Concept Of Marriage
759-B	Torah Concept Of Marriage
1209	Harmony In The Home (Part 1)
1210	Harmony In The Home (Part 2)
1236	How Marriage Helps Us Realize Our Potential
1440	The Torah Concept Of Marriage
1512	For Kallahs
1655	The Foundation Of Marriage
1699	Lecture To Kallahs

FOR MEN

618	The Man's Role In A Jewish Family
1080	Lecture For Chassanim (5 Parts—A-E)
1550	Man's Role In Marriage
1559	For Men Only
1597	The Man's Role In Marriage

FOR WOMEN

100	In The Merit Of Righteous Women We Were Redeemed..
546	Kidush Hashem By Women
613	The Woman's Role In The Family
620	"Man And Woman He Created Them"
623	The Woman's Role In Judaism
625	A Happy Jewish Family
651	Woman's Role In Building The Bais Hamikdash
1087	Lecture For Kallahs
1296	The Meaning Of Marriage
1304	The Woman's Role In Marriage
1598	The Woman's Role In Marriage

FOR GIRLS

108	For A Girl—Leaving Egypt
709	Role Of A Jewish Girl
845	Let's Care For Each Other (The 3 Weeks)
1057	My Role In Creation
1135	Appreciate Being Chosen
1374	For The Seminary Girl
1702	Chessed Of A Bas Yisroel

AUDIO TAPES BY RABBI EZRIEL TAUBER

PARSHA

80	Parshas Bereishis
1493	The Man As A Tree (Bereishis)
1286	The Significance Of The Binding Of Yizchok (Vayaira)
1283	Know Who You Are (Vayaira)
1495	Akaidas Yitzchok Today (Vayaira)
1288	Sarah's Life, All Good (Chayai Sara)
921	Yaakov's Purchase Of Esav's Bechorah (Toldos)
1509	How To Ask Hashem (Toldos)
153	Parshas Vayeitsei
95	Parshas Vayechi
168	Be Like Ephraim And Menasha (Vayechi)
635	The Bush Burning In Fire (Va'Ara)
119	Parshas Yisro-Mishpotim
1556	Build Me A Sanctuary (Truma)
192	Make Your Own Luchos (Ki Sisa)
1564	Half Shekel Or Golden Calf (Ki Sisa)
195	Women's Participation In Building Of The Mishkan (Pekudai)
666	Benefits Of The Jewish Dietary Laws (Shmini)
695	Parshas Hameraglim (Shlach)
1602	No Reason To Fear (Shlach)
1605	The Only Medicine Today (Shlach)
1608	Parshas Shlach
1611	Not To Be Like Korach—Today
1614	Parshas Chukas
245	Listen And Then Realize (R'ah)

MISCELLANEOUS

266	The Role Of Our Mother Rachel
517-A	The Definition Of Truth
517-B	The Definition Of Truth
557	Should We Be Exposed To The World
630	Fashion—The Uniform Of A Goy
632	Multiple Plans In The Universe
752	Love Hashem
755	Curiosity—Why?
787	To Combat Proudness
833	One Solution For All Problems
840	Live For The Present
847	Discover Your Wisdom
851	Questions And Answers
857	The Meaning Of Chessed
863	Tranquility
907	Prophecies In Our Times
915	Questions And Answers
927	Money As Eternity
944	We As Survivors
948	Develop The Right Desire
964	You Cannot Dilute The Truth
966-A	Codes In The Torah
966-B	Codes In The Torah
967	Prophecies Materialized In Our Times
1021	Achievements Of Positive Thinking
1094	Getting Things Done
1097	The Definition Of Truth
1148	Honoring Parents
1185	Questions & Answers
1187	Justify Your Consumption
1190	Questions & Answers
1211	Remembering
1321	How To Find A Friend
1341-A	Codes In The Torah
1341-B	Codes In The Torah
1412	Think Right
1449	Thoughtfulness—Patch Of Relationships
1451	Let's Start Thinking
1460	Free Will Vs. Fate
1520	Three Conditions To Chassidus
1527	How To Acquire Chassidus
1542	The Ladder Of Shovevim
1543	Holocaust And Zionism
1544	Learning The Truth From Falsehood
1545	Chizuk
1546	The Importance Of Unity
1580	Self Discover Truth
1592	Find Your Greatness In Your Nothingness

AUDIO TAPES
BY RABBI EZRIEL TAUBER

1600	Know How Important You Are	524	The Marriage Of Israel And Hashem
1609	Questions And Answers	646	Shira Before Torah
1612	Why Not Seek Help By Mystics	682	Let's Do And Listen
1634	Ten Steps To Growth	824	The Development Of Man
1638	Recapture Yourself	829	The Essence Of Torah
1670	The Value Of A Moment	1200	The Gift Of Torah
1674	Mitzvas Yichud Hashem (Advanced)	1201	My Share In Torah
		1395	Preparation For Torah
1675	How To Enjoy Every Moment	1402	My Personal Torah
1676	Eretz Yisrael Is Acquired Through Pain		

THE THREE WEEKS & TISHA B'AV

PESACH

		125	Mourn With Joy
		127	Torah Never Went To Golus
207	Do Not Rebel Against The Nations	566	The Golden Calf
		569	Building The Bais Hamikdash With Our Fire
209	The Four Parshiyos		
654	Belief And Knowledge	704	I, As A Walking Bais Hamikdash
659	Be Aware Of Our Times		
661	Split Your Own Sea	708	Selfless Love
796	Be A Proud Jew	843	Let's Build The Third Bais Hamikdash
979	Enthusiasm For Pesach		
1170	Leaving Egypt Today	849	Make Use Of Your Intellect
1180	Our Crucial Days	855	Let's Represent G-D
1317	Self Appreciation	858	Life As A Service To Hashem
1381	Uplifting Pesach Thoughts	859	Me, As A Torch Of Life
1392	Celebrate Your Birthday	1019	Build Your Bais Hamikdash
1568	Pesach	1023	Turning Sadness Into Joy
1723	The Process Of Growth	1028	The Birthday Of Moshiach
		1221	Today's Bais Hamikdash
		1226	Rebuild The Bais Hamikdash
		1228	True Value Vs. Symbolic Value

SFIRAS HA'OMER

48	Are You Proud To Be A Jew?	1233	You As A Bais Hamikdash
110	Sefira, In Our Time	1226	Rebuild The Bais Hamikdash
226	Humbleness—An Ingredient To Happiness	1228	True Value Vs. Symbolic Value
543	Responsibility—Collectively And Individually	1233	You As A Bais Hamikdash
		1462	Let's Meet Hashem
678	Rabbi Akiva's Disciples	1626	How To Build The Bais Hamikdash
810	To Be High—Or Money		
819	The Real World	1627	How To Prepare For Life
993	Victorious Israel	1628	The Birth Of Moshiach
1186	My Personal Growth	1630	Have I Done My Share? (Tisha B'Av)
1192	We, As Rabbi Akiva's Talmidim		
		1631	Shabbos Chazon—Nachmu
1398	The Message Of Rabbi Akiva		
1585	My Mission		

ELUL

SHAVUOS

		72	From The Depths I Call Out To You, Hashem
220	Creation At Matan Torah		

AUDIO TAPES
BY RABBI EZRIEL TAUBER

132	Mechanics Of Teshuva	894	The Real Truth
135	Real Chessed		
136	Teshuva With Simcha		**CHANUKAH**
249	Teshuva With Shofar		
261	My Only Request Of Hashem	161	The Eternal Light
446	Be An Original Jew	271	Chanuka, 5745
600	Meaning Of The Akaidah	746	Bring Chanukah
711	Fill In Your Time	920	Why Are We Hated
719	Obtaining Love Of Hashem	926	Me As Hashem's Candle
720	Choose Life	935	Mizvas Yediah—Emunah
862	Truth	939	Me As A Chanukah-Light
864	In The Book Of Life	1295	The Four Goluses
1033	The Advantage Of Elul	1306	Surprises About Chanukah
1039	The Concealed Power In You	1310	Bayomim Hohaim Bizman Hazeh
1048	My Resolution		
1265	A Full Jew	1515	Chanuka
1470	What Is There For Us To Give?	1518	Self Esteem
		1690	Kindle Your Own Flame
1472	What Are We Giving To Hashem?	1691	To Thank And To Praise
1643	Elul		**PURIM**

	ROSH HASHANNAH	105	How To Oppose Amalek And Pharaoh
718	Two Ways Of Praying	777	Fight Amalek
867	What Can I Give To Hashem?	779	Develop Simcha
869	Let's Be Honest	784	Enjoying The Golus
876	Corronate Hashem	792	The Homon Of Today
878	Make Me King	793	Mordechai And Esther Today
1034	Let's Corronate Hashem	797	Egypt In Our Times
1035	I, As A Representative Of Hashem	971	How To Generate Simcha
		972	Assimilating Whilst Religious
1055	Power Of Prayer	974	Pesach—Purim—Pesach
1259	Please Corronate Me	1159	How Is Amalek Effecting Us
1642	The Gift Of Rosh Hashono	1344	A Successful Simcha
		1359	Revelation Of Yisroel
	YOM KIPPUR	1377	Opportunities You Might Miss
		1557	Pharaoh-Amalek/Purim-Pesach
722	Take Yom Kippur With You	1561	Getting Rid Of Amalek
881	Join Me Totally	1562	The End Of Amalek
883	Do It For Your Name	1719	How To Develop Simcha
1061	The Mitzvah In Teshuva	1720	Simcha Against Amalek
1480	I Am Ready For Trial		
1482	Corronate Me		**TAPE SERIES**
1483	Chessed, All The Time		
1647	My Real Identity		
1650	Let's Thank Hashem		

Chovas Halevavos (100 Tapes)
Maharal—Netzach Yisroel (53 Tapes)
Maharal—Nesiv Hateshuva (18 Tapes)

SUCCOS

Maharal—Gevuros Hashem (70 Tapes, more upcoming)

603	Decoration To G–D
890	The Meaning Of Simcha

Maharal—On The Haggadah (15 Tapes)
Maharal—Rosh Hashannah (3 Tapes)

AUDIO TAPES
BY RABBI EZRIEL TAUBER

Maharal—Ohr Chodosh (3 Tapes)
Ramchal—Daas Tevunos (73 Tapes)
Ramchal—Derech Hashem (7 Tapes)
Ramchal—Mesilas Yeshorim (62 Tapes)
Tefillah (4 Tapes)
Shir Hashirim (12 Tapes)
Koheles (29 Tapes)
Tanya (52 Tapes)
Series Of Tapes For Chassanim (5 Tapes)
Series Of Tapes For Kallahs—Various Speakers (6 Tapes)

TAPE SERIES FOR SPECIAL GROUPS

Series Of Lectures For Divorcees
Series Of Lectures For Childless Couples
Series Of Lectures For Single Girls
Series Of Lectures For Widows
Series Of Lectures For Bereaved Parents

YIDDISH

Chovos Halevavos (51 Tapes)
Tanya (30 Tapes)
Bechol Derochechah Daihu (10 Tapes)
Series Of Tapes For Chassanim (5 Tapes)
Ramchal—Mesilas Yeshorim (8 Tapes)
Ramchal—Derech Hashem (12 Tapes)
Maharal—Tiferes Yisroel (52 Tapes)
Maharal—Netzach Yisroel (25 Tapes)
Maharal—Derech Chaim (19 Tapes)
Maharal—Gevuros Hashem (14 Tapes)
Maharal—Nesiv Hatorah (9 Tapes)

HEBREW

Chovos Helevavos (86 Tapes)

Parshas Hashovua (81 Tapes)
Shir Hashirim (7 Tapes)
Tefillah (30 Tapes)
Ramchal—Mesilas Yeshorim (25 Tapes)
Ramchal—Mamar Haikrim (6 Tapes)
Ramchal—Derech Etz Chaim (7 Tapes)

VIDEOS

1. Hidden Codes In The Torah
2. Soul Searching (With Dr. Brian Weiss)
3. The Definition Of Truth
4. Creation And Its Purpose
5. Definition Of Life
6. Torah Concept Of Marriage
7. Harmony And Peace In The Jewish Home
8. "Golus"—The Benefit Of Suffering
9. Panel Discussion—Questions And Answers
10. The Significance Of Torah And Tefillah
11. The Meaning Of Shabbos
12. Prophecies Materialized In Our Times
13. Effort And Bitachon Towards Making A Living
14. Improving
15. Practicality In Day To Day Life
16. Choose Life
17. "We Are One"—Why And How
18. Us In Creation
19. Tranquility In Business

BOOKS BY RABBI EZRIEL TAUBER
(Prices are for hardcover editions)

I Shall Not Want—finding optimal meaning in the work you do
$12

To Become One—the making of a successful marriage
$13

Choose Life!—powerful lessons how to live life to the utmost
$16

Days Are Coming—the modern world as reflective of age-old prophecies
$16

Darkness Before Dawn—the Holocaust and individual suffering
$18

Self-Esteem—paths to personal growth
$18

Beyond Survival—the foundations of living a well-rounded, spiritual life
$13